ESSENTIALS OF

Consensual
Qualitative Research

Essentials of Qualitative Methods Series

ESSENTIALS OF

Consensual Qualitative Research

Clara E. Hill
Sarah Knox

 AMERICAN PSYCHOLOGICAL ASSOCIATION

Published by
American Psychological Association
750 First Street, NE
Washington, DC 20002
https://www.apa.org

Order Department
https://www.apa.org/pubs/books
order@apa.org

In the U.K., Europe, Africa, and the Middle East, copies may be ordered from Eurospan
https://www.eurospanbookstore.com/apa
info@eurospangroup.com

Typeset in Charter by Circle Graphics, Inc., Reisterstown, MD

Printer: Sheridan Books, Chelsea, MI
Cover Designer: Anne Kerns, Anne Likes Red, Silver Spring, MD

Library of Congress Cataloging-in-Publication Data

Names: Hill, Clara E., 1948- author. | Knox, Sarah (Psychologist) author.
Title: Essentials of consensual qualitative research / Clara E. Hill and Sarah Knox.
Description: Washington : American Psychological Association, 2021. |
Series: Essentials of qualitative methods | Includes bibliographical references
   and index.
Identifiers: LCCN 2020021143 (print) | LCCN 2020021144 (ebook) |
   ISBN 9781433833458 (paperback) | ISBN 9781433833465 (ebook)
Subjects: LCSH: Qualitative research. | Psychology—Qualitative research. |
   Social sciences—Research. | Social sciences—Methodology.
Classification: LCC H62 .H5115 2021 (print) | LCC H62 (ebook) |
   DDC 300.72/1—dc23
LC record available at https://lccn.loc.gov/2020021143
LC ebook record available at https://lccn.loc.gov/2020021144

https://doi.org/10.1037/0000215-000

Printed in the United States of America

10 9 8 7 6 5 4 3 2 1

Contents

Series Foreword

Qualitative approaches have become accepted and indeed embraced as empirical methods within the social sciences, as scholars have realized that many of the phenomena in which we are interested are complex and require deep inner reflection and equally penetrating examination. Quantitative approaches often cannot capture such phenomena well through their standard methods (e.g., self-report measures), so qualitative designs using interviews and other in-depth data-gathering procedures offer exciting, nimble, and useful research approaches.

Indeed, the number and variety of qualitative approaches that have been developed is remarkable. We remember Bill Stiles saying (quoting Chairman Mao) at one meeting about methods, "Let a hundred flowers bloom," indicating that there are many appropriate methods for addressing research questions. In this series, we celebrate this diversity (hence, the cover design of flowers).

The question for many of us, though, has been how to decide among approaches and how to learn the different methods. Many prior descriptions of the various qualitative methods have not provided clear enough descriptions of the methods, making it difficult for novice researchers to learn how to use them. Thus, those interested in learning about and pursuing qualitative research need crisp and thorough descriptions of these approaches, with lots of examples to illustrate the method so that readers can grasp how to use the methods.

The purpose of this series of books, then, is to present a range of different qualitative approaches that seemed most exciting and illustrative of the range of methods appropriate for social science research. We asked leading experts in qualitative methods to contribute to the series, and we were delighted that they accepted our invitation. Through this series, readers have the opportunity to learn qualitative research methods from those who developed the methods and/or who have been using them successfully for years.

We asked the authors of each book to provide context for the method, including a rationale, situating the method within the qualitative tradition, describing the method's philosophical and epistemological background, and noting the key features of the method. We then asked them to describe in detail the steps of the method, including the research team, sampling, biases and expectations, data collection, data analysis, and variations on the method. We also asked authors to provide tips for the research process and for writing a manuscript emerging from a study that used the method. Finally, we asked authors to reflect on the methodological integrity of the approach, along with the benefits and limitations of the particular method.

This series of books can be used in several different ways. Instructors teaching courses in qualitative research could use the whole series, presenting one method at a time as they expose students to a range of qualitative methods. Alternatively, instructors could choose to focus on just a few approaches, as depicted in specific books, supplementing the books with examples from studies that have been published using the approaches, and providing experiential exercises to help students get started using the approaches.

In this particular book, we present consensual qualitative research, or CQR, a method that was first written about in Hill et al. (1997) and has since been widely used, especially by psychotherapy researchers. The main features of this approach are the use of a research team and auditors, consensus among judges, and a high emphasis on rigor and replicability. CQR is ideal for studying inner experiences, attitudes, and beliefs.

—Clara E. Hill and Sarah Knox

ESSENTIALS OF
Consensual
Qualitative Research

1 CONCEPTUAL FOUNDATIONS OF CONSENSUAL QUALITATIVE RESEARCH

Consensual qualitative research (CQR) is a qualitative method that can be used to study inner experiences, attitudes, and beliefs, all of which are not readily observable. Although we have used CQR primarily in psychotherapy research, it has also been used to study a variety of other topics, such as culture (e.g., Tuason et al., 2007), career development (Schaefer et al., 2004), trauma (Gali Cinamon & Hason, 2009), medical and health-related areas (e.g., Brown et al., 2008), same-sex relationships (Sánchez et al., 2009), and study abroad experiences (Bikos et al., 2019). Hence, CQR is widely applicable to topics in education and the behavioral and social sciences (e.g., social justice, urban leadership development, effects of teachers on students, parenting).

We first formally presented CQR more than 20 years ago (Hill et al., 1997). We then provided an update (Hill et al., 2005) and an edited book (Hill, 2012). The time now seemed ripe for an even further-updated and clearer version with more examples. This new book is particularly suited for researchers new to CQR because we distill the most important information on the method and provide practical tips. So, if you are interested in studying such things as banter in psychotherapy, authenticity in high school students, burnout in medical professionals, or difficulties navigating being a mother and professor during a pandemic, CQR is an ideal method because researchers can interview people to find out in-depth information that cannot easily be found using traditional experimental and quantitative methods.

SITUATING CQR WITHIN THE QUALITATIVE TRADITION

Rather than situating CQR within all qualitative traditions (see instead McLeod, 2011), we review the approaches that most influenced us as psychotherapy researchers in developing CQR. I (Clara Hill) was trained in quantitative methods, as were most psychologists before 1980. The first movement in psychotherapy research toward more qualitative methods involved discovery-oriented or exploratory approaches (Elliott, 1984; Hill, 1990; Mahrer, 1988). Mahrer (1988), for example, highlighted the limitations of hypothesis testing (i.e., quantitative approaches) for advancing knowledge about psychotherapy and suggested instead that

> researchers adopt the rationale, aims, and methods of discovery-oriented psychotherapy research . . . [because] the whole basis for designing discovery-oriented studies is the intention to learn more; to be surprised; to find out what one does not already expect, predict, or hypothesize; to answer a question whose answer provides something one wants to know but might not have expected, predicted, or hypothesized. (p. 697)

In Mahrer's discovery-oriented method, a team of judges develops categories based on the data for that study (discovers what the data offer rather than applying an existing measure or conceptualization to the data). Once the categories are well developed, researchers train a new team of judges to independently code the same data into the categories, requiring high interrater reliability among all judges. Despite his advocacy for discovery-oriented approaches, Mahrer thus still retained many positivist elements in his emerging qualitative method, specifically in requiring high interrater reliability among judges.

The next qualitative approaches that developed within psychology and psychotherapy research were phenomenological approaches (Giorgi, 1985), comprehensive process analysis (CPA; Elliott, 1989), and grounded theory (GT; Strauss & Corbin, 1990). These qualitative methods rely on judges examining data (usually words, narratives, stories) from an inductive stance (rather than a hypothesis testing stance). Although these methods have been used widely, their steps often seemed vague, difficult to understand, and difficult to implement. Given our desire to create a rigorous approach that could be easily taught and used, we sought to integrate the best features of the existing approaches (i.e., discovery oriented, exploratory, phenomenological, CPA, GT) into CQR (Hill, 2012; Hill et al., 1997, 2005).

PHILOSOPHICAL UNDERPINNINGS OF CQR

CQR is "predominantly constructivist, with some post-positivist elements" (Hill et al., 2005, p. 197). CQR researchers rely on naturalistic and interactive methods, consistent with constructivist approaches. Thus, CQR researchers explore a phenomenon as it naturally occurs (rather than altering or manipulating it) and typically interact with participants via data-gathering interviews. They derive the meaning of the phenomenon under examination from participants' words and text and also attend to the context of participants' words (e.g., under what circumstances did the phenomenon occur?). They gather rich data by using probes and clarifications (Hill et al., 2005; Ponterotto, 2005).

Ontologically (i.e., a view of the nature of reality), CQR researchers acknowledge the existence of multiple, equally valid, socially constructed versions of the "truth" (a constructivist view). Thus, researchers embrace the uniqueness of each participant's experience while also exploring potential commonalities of experiences across participants.

CQR also has features of postpositivism in the pursuit of consensus among team members and auditors, with team members working collaboratively to co-construct the best representation of the data by integrating multiple perspectives (Ponterotto, 2005). Using these multiple perspectives, in conjunction with constantly returning to the raw data, researchers explore and try to reflect the complexity of the data. Furthermore, including auditors in the consensus process minimizes groupthink and provides an additional perspective to aid the team in hearing other views so that they can best represent the data (Hill, 2012; Hill et al., 1997). This emphasis on consensus differentiates CQR from other qualitative approaches that rely primarily on a single researcher's interpretation of the data.

Epistemologically, CQR researchers are predominantly constructivist in their acknowledgment of the mutual influence of researcher and participant. In CQR, interviewers learn about the phenomenon from the participants and also help the participants explore their experiences of that phenomenon more deeply. The postpositivist component of CQR's epistemology lies in the use of a standard, semistructured interview protocol to obtain consistent information across participants, thus ensuring that the same set of foundational questions is asked of all participants. Interviewers, however, also probe participants' responses deeply during interviews to gain in-depth, unique data about the individual participant's experiences. This type of interview protocol differs from more constructivist methods, where protocols evolve as the research progresses. We consider such evolving protocols problematic because participants may not be responding to the same foundational questions, thereby leading to inconsistent data collection across participants.

In terms of the researcher's values (axiology), the CQR approach again includes elements of both constructivism and postpositivism. In CQR, we acknowledge that researchers' biases are inevitable and should be discussed and acknowledged openly (a constructivist approach); we also assert that these biases can be bracketed (i.e., set aside) somewhat to minimize the influence of biases on the results. In CQR, we aim to represent how participants (not researchers) view the world, and the assumption is that with bracketing, different teams would understand the data similarly as they discern the meaning of the data themselves rather than their perspective on the data. As we analyze the data, we seek to become aware of our biases and are transparent in presenting them to readers so that they can evaluate the results on the basis of knowing our biases. Furthermore, CQR researchers all use the same interview protocol to reduce the potential effect of individual interviewers (a postpositivistic approach), but we duly recognize that biases nevertheless influence how we conduct interviews (e.g., researchers may pursue some topics more or less deeply depending on their interests or experiences) and interpret the data (e.g., researchers may see different things in the data depending on their perspectives). These potential influences are also minimized by an open discussion of the researchers' biases and expectations.

Finally, CQR's rhetorical structure (i.e., writing style) has postpositivist elements, given that we try to present results as objectively as possible (their findings can be traced directly to the raw data), avoid broad interpretations, and report findings in the third person. Furthermore, the goal is to discover themes across participants so that results can be transferred to a larger population (Hill et al., 2005; Ponterotto, 2005). Constructivist features, however, are found in the use of quotations to illustrate the lived experience (Ponterotto, 2005).

RATIONALE FOR USING CQR

CQR is ideal for studying in depth the experiences (e.g., misunderstandings), attitudes (e.g., attitudes about racism), and beliefs (e.g., beliefs about social justice) of individuals because it allows researchers to gain a rich, detailed understanding that is not usually possible with quantitative methods (e.g., such measures often constrain participants' responses). CQR is also particularly useful for investigations of inner events (e.g., secrets, internal responses to an intervention) about which participants may have ambivalent or suppressed feelings that cannot easily be observed by outsiders. People often need time and an interested listener to be able to delve into their thoughts and feelings about such complex and emotionally charged topics. In addition, CQR can be used to study events that occur infrequently (e.g., weeping) or at variable time points (e.g., changes in mood) because these are often hard for researchers to find and examine quantitatively. Perhaps most important, CQR is useful for topics that have not been studied previously and thus for which there are no psychometrically sound measures available.

Although we are admitted advocates for CQR, we do not argue that researchers should use only qualitative approaches in their investigations, but rather that researchers should choose the approach that best fits their research question. For example, if the researcher's intent is to investigate the outcomes of two different psychotherapeutic approaches, a quantitative clinical trials method involving standardized measures and statistical analyses is better suited than a qualitative approach. A qualitative approach, however, would be better suited to answering questions about how participants experienced the two different approaches because it would allow the participants to think deeply about their experiences. Furthermore, it is often useful to include a qualitative component in largely quantitative studies to provide a richer understanding of the phenomenon. Furthermore, mixed methods (i.e., combining quantitative and qualitative) approaches often provide valuable data about the same phenomenon from different perspectives.

KEY FEATURES OF CQR

Exhibit 1.1 shows the key features of CQR. In this book, we focus on CQR as applied through interviews, although we describe variations of CQR in Chapter 8.

The following is a quick overview of CQR. Researchers first organize interview data within cases (i.e., participants) into domains (topic areas). For each case, they then summarize data within domains into core ideas (which restate the interview data in clearer, simpler terms). Finally, they conduct a cross-analysis in which they construct categories and subcategories (representing themes) within domains across cases to characterize the common patterns in the findings.

EXHIBIT 1.1. Key Features of CQR

1. Assumption: Data are constructed (there is no objective truth).

2. Underlying principles
   a. The method is inductive (bottom-up data analysis) rather than deductive.
   b. We use open-ended questions (i.e., opening up the interviewee to explore and think) rather than closed questions (i.e., ask for specific information or facts).
   c. Data involve words, narratives, and stories rather than numbers.
   d. Context is important to understand the data.
   e. We gather rich in-depth data on a small number of participants.
   f. We use multiple perspectives (i.e., research team, auditor[s]) to understand the data.
   g. We try to be aware of and bracket (set aside) our biases and expectations.
   h. We use consensus among team members to resolve differences of opinion.
   i. We continually return to the raw data to check our understandings.

3. Data analysis method
   a. Within cases, the research team divides data into domains (topic areas).
   b. Within cases, the research team develops core ideas (summaries) for all ideas.
   c. Auditors check the domains and core ideas for each case.
   d. Across cases, we look for themes and patterns (conduct a cross-analysis).
   e. Auditors check the cross-analysis.

In terms of our assumptions, we first acknowledge that the data elicited in CQR are constructed. In other words, we recognize that there is no objective truth for the phenomena we are investigating. Thus, rather than striving to prove whether what someone says is accurate, we are more interested in hearing about participants' experiences and perceptions.

In CQR, data analysis is inductive or bottom-up (observing and describing a phenomenon and then drawing conclusions from these data) rather than top-down (imposing a theoretical lens on the data or setting out to confirm or disconfirm hypotheses). In other words, researchers allow the results to emerge organically from the data, imposing as few theoretical constructs on the data as possible. For example, rather than testing whether therapist self-disclosure leads to client disclosure and insight (and only measuring those potential outcomes), researchers might ask clients how they respond to therapist self-disclosure and then examine systematically the consequences that emerge. In this way, CQR researchers are open to uncovering new and unexpected findings rather than just setting out to prove what they had anticipated and measured. Thus, CQR researchers typically formulate and explore research questions rather than hypotheses.

A related key feature is the use of open-ended questions for collecting data. Researchers ask participants to say whatever comes to mind in response to open questions about the topic (e.g., "What was your experience of your supervisor at that moment?") without imposing predetermined ideas about their experiences (e.g., "Did you feel angry?").

In addition, CQR relies on words, narratives, and stories as data, rather than numbers. As noted earlier, researchers allow participants to talk about what they are thinking or feeling, asking for a full description of experiences related to the topic rather than trying to capture such experiences through a numerical rating on a scale. We also explore what words mean to the participant rather than imposing our meaning on the words (e.g., "Tell me more about the feelings of abandonment you just mentioned").

Furthermore, context is crucial for understanding the participant's experience. Thus, researchers have to be immersed (i.e., fully involved) in everything the person has said before interpreting the data. For example, knowing that the participant is divorced may provide important context for understanding the participant's attitudes toward marriage.

Yet another key feature is the reliance on small samples of participants studied in depth, rather than collecting superficial data from a large number of participants. Researchers thus attempt to recruit a small number of participants who can speak articulately and deeply about their experiences. Assuming that the sample is relatively homogeneous (i.e., similar on relevant variables), the data are likely to be saturated (i.e., reach a point where minimal further information is gained by adding participants) with a sample of 13 to 15.

Because of the inherent biases in this process of making meaning out of people's stories (it is often difficult for people to articulate their experiences, and researchers' perspectives inevitably influence their understanding of others' experiences), another key feature is the use of multiple perspectives to analyze the data. Thus, we use a primary team of three to four researchers, along with one to two auditors, all of whom listen carefully and respectfully to everyone's perspective to make sure we get a nuanced and rich understanding of the data.

In addition, we individually try to be aware of and bracket (set aside) our biases and expectations because we recognize that these can unduly influence data collection and analysis. We reflect on these biases and expectations and share them with the research team in hopes that we can be aware and accountable to each other when issues inevitably arise about our personal responses to the topic. Likewise, we write about our biases and expectations in research publications so that readers can be aware of them and evaluate results accordingly.

Next, *consensus*, which can be defined as an unforced unanimous decision (Schielke et al., 2009), is an integral part of CQR, as its name suggests. During the consensus process, researchers review the data independently and then discuss their ideas until all members of the team agree on the best representation of the data (Hill et al., 1997). Thus, researchers seek a common understanding of the data that respects individual team members' perspectives and "relies on mutual respect, equal involvement, and shared power" (Hill et al., 1997, p. 523). The consensus process is central to the credibility or trustworthiness of the data analysis because it allows us to triangulate different researchers' understanding of the data. If multiple people agree on an interpretation, researchers have more confidence that others would agree with that interpretation (Schielke et al., 2009) than they would if only one person analyzed and interpreted the data (Morrow, 2005). Furthermore, research has suggested that "unforced consensus may result in interpretations that are deeper, richer, and more thorough, precise, and realistic than one generated by a single individual" (Schielke et al., 2009, p. 559).

The final key feature of CQR is returning to the raw data to ensure that the emerging understanding of the data is grounded in participants' words. When team members disagree on how they view data, for example, they reread the participant's words, listen to a recording of the interview, and think about the context of the case to help them determine whether their interpretation of the data arises from the data or their own biases and expectations.

CONCLUSIONS

We developed CQR from our experiences with quantitatively based psychotherapy process research (e.g., discovery-oriented and exploratory methods) and also from other qualitative methods (GT, phenomenology, and CPA). It is a rigorous method oriented to helping researchers gain in-depth information about topics related to inner experiences, attitudes, and beliefs from a few carefully recruited participants. Multiple voices are encouraged to help researchers hear different perspectives and think deeply about the data.

2 GETTING STARTED

In this chapter, we cover several steps to help researchers using consensual qualitative research (CQR) launch their projects. We present the steps in the order in which researchers usually proceed in the initial phase of projects: selecting the topic, reviewing the literature, constructing research questions, identifying a population, and selecting a research team and auditors.

SELECTING THE TOPIC

It is important to choose a topic in which you have a strong interest. Because CQR projects often take a year or more to complete, only a personally fascinating topic is likely to sustain motivation and momentum throughout the process. Potential topics often emerge from researchers' experiences with various phenomena (e.g., having experienced therapist advice as therapists and clients, researchers may wonder how other therapists use the intervention and how other clients respond to it). We caution, however, that it can be hard if you are so invested in obtaining a particular result that you struggle to remain open to what the data show. For example, it may be difficult to

https://doi.org/10.1037/0000215-002
Essentials of Consensual Qualitative Research, by C. E. Hill and S. Knox

investigate a special education program that you developed and are passionate about "proving" and then disseminating.

Researchers also should be careful to pick topics that are, on the one hand, important and meaningful enough to study but, on the other hand, not so grandiose and vague that they cannot be examined. An illustration is the topic of clients' emotional experiences in therapy, which is interesting but broad. It would be more manageable to focus, for example, on client experiences of crying in therapy.

REVIEWING THE LITERATURE

Some (e.g., Glaser, 1978; Shank, 2002) have argued that qualitative researchers should be familiar enough with the literature to determine whether their proposed study has already been conducted but should not review the literature completely until after the data have been collected. This assertion is based on the idea that qualitative researchers must put aside preconceived notions and use an exploratory approach in analyzing their data.

In contrast, we (Hill et al., 1997) have argued that awareness of the literature helps researchers build on existing knowledge and avoid missteps experienced by prior investigators. Reviewing the literature also enables researchers to become familiar with concepts and relationships that other researchers have identified in previous studies and thus consider the role that such concepts or relationships might play in their project.

Although we advocate reviewing the extant literature to design the study, we suggest that researchers using CQR bracket (i.e., set aside) such knowledge when interviewing participants and analyzing the data so they can approach the data openly with a fresh and unbiased perspective. In this way, researchers allow the data to "speak" for themselves, which often yields unexpected results (Hill et al., 1997).

WRITING A PROPOSAL AND CONSTRUCTING RESEARCH QUESTIONS

We suggest that researchers using CQR write a proposal about what they plan to do in their study, even when the study is not a student project, because thinking clearly ahead of time strengthens the study design. This proposal would involve developing your rationale for the study, briefly reviewing the extant literature and discerning what is missing from that literature, and stating the purpose of your study along with two to three primary research questions.

For the research questions (i.e., those that guide or serve as the foundation for the entire study), we try to be as specific as possible (e.g., "How do new faculty navigate the transition from graduate school to their first professional position?" "How do first-time parents cope with the transition to parenthood?"). We recognize, of course, that our research questions will probably change as we create our interview protocol and do pilot interviews, but identifying them at this point provides focus and direction for the study.

Note that we do not develop hypotheses (e.g., "Students will gain self-efficacy from participating in a study-abroad program"). Rather, we want to remain open to allowing unexpected findings to emerge from the data and to learning from the participants.

IDENTIFYING THE POPULATION

In conjunction with constructing research questions, we have to identify the target population (i.e., the entire group from which a sample is selected). Our goal is to define our population clearly, so we know to whom the results apply. Although there is some controversy about the construct of generalizability in qualitative research, we believe that researchers using CQR do indeed want to apply their findings, at least tentatively, beyond their sample (called *transferability* in qualitative research), and so identifying the appropriate population and then sampling from it (covered in the next chapter) is crucial.

One of the main considerations is choosing a population that fits the research questions (i.e., they have experienced the phenomenon under investigation). Those who are interviewed must be knowledgeable about and able to share experiences related to the topic at hand. For example, in their study of transference, Gelso et al. (1999) identified that they were interested in psychoanalytically oriented psychotherapists who understood the concept of transference, had thought deeply about transference, and had experienced transference themselves as clients and therapists. In contrast, Hill et al. (1996) wanted to learn from therapists from any theoretical orientation about their experiences of working with impasses in psychotherapy. The different research questions thus guided the choice of the population.

In defining the population, researchers should also consider demographic variables that might be relevant to the research question(s), such as gender, age, sexual orientation, socioeconomic status, racial or ethnic status, country of residence, religion, disability status, and educational level. Thus, if we were studying the effects of psychotherapy with clients who have experienced trauma, we might be concerned with gender, race, ethnicity, socioeconomic status, and type of trauma, given that trauma might occur differentially and have different outcomes across groups. We might then decide to select only upper-class African American men who had been sexually abused so that we know the population to which we are referring.

Also of particular relevance is choosing a population for whom the experience was relatively recent. If interviewers are asking psychotherapy clients about a fleeting experience of feeling understood in a therapy session, it is probably best to interview clients immediately after sessions so that details are clear in the clients' minds. Otherwise, participants are likely to "fill in the gaps" and not remember the experience as clearly.

However, some events might be especially powerful or salient and may thus be clearly remembered even years later. The problem, however, is that feelings about the event may change over time. For example, if the research question involves a perspective on the grieving process after the death of a child, researchers should carefully consider what the grieving process would look like immediately after the death, a year later, 2 to 5 years later, and 5 to 10 years later. Researchers in such a study would have to determine the time frame they are most interested in because they might have too broad a range of results if they did not specify or narrow the time frame (researchers of such a study might also want to consider other variables that could influence the results, including type of death, age of child, and religion of parents).

SELECTING, TRAINING, AND WORKING WITH THE RESEARCH TEAM

The research team carries out the data collection and data analyses, so choosing a good team is crucial. Moreover, auditors monitor the process and also have to be chosen carefully.

Selecting the Research Team

We suggest that you select people who are willing and able to make a major commitment of time, actively participate, and voice their opinions as team members. Hill et al. (1997) suggested that research team members should have good interpersonal skills, be open to feedback, and be motivated to work on interpersonal relationships.

Another consideration when selecting team members is level of experience, which can include familiarity with the subject being studied, prior involvement on a CQR team, or experience with research in general. Experienced team members are typically more desirable for subjects that require specific knowledge or training (e.g., countertransference; Hayes et al., 1998), whereas less experienced undergraduates are often quite able to participate as team members for research on topics that may not demand such prior knowledge (e.g., women's career development; Williams et al., 1998).

Selecting team members who add diversity can also be beneficial. For instance, including members who have different educational or cultural backgrounds can add to the richness of team discussions. Decisions about the diversity or homogeneity of the research team should be considered, in part, based on the research topic. For example, if researchers are studying heterosexual marital relationships, having both male and female team members might enable the team to better understand both gender perspectives.

If research team members will also serve as interviewers, it is essential to select people who can conduct a good interview. Interviewers have to be empathic listeners who can gently and competently elicit information from participants. For our research teams, we typically seek individuals who have at least had a class in basic counseling skills (e.g., learning about open-ended questions and paraphrases). Such training helps potential interviewers understand the purpose of using these skills in interviews, how these skills affect interviewees, and the type of information to be gathered by using these skills. In short, trained interviewers can be more intentional during interviews, thus yielding more in-depth information from the interviews.

Organizational psychologists (West, 2004) have suggested that team members must have a shared goal or vision to obtain rich data that honor the experiences of the participants and add to the knowledge base of the field. West also suggested that team members must feel a commitment to the team in agreeing to the meeting times and the anticipated duration of the project. Finally, West noted that establishing and maintaining trust in the research group is important so that members feel open to sharing their thoughts and opinions.

Differences in power among team members may influence the team process (see also Hill, 2012). As an illustration, when teams are composed of faculty members (who have more social power) and students (who have less social power), students may be reluctant, especially initially, to voice their opinions due to concerns about alienating their advisors or mentors or because of deference to authority. As noted later, however, faculty team members can work to create an open and nonthreatening environment so that all members feel comfortable voicing their thoughts, regardless of their social power. We stress that people at all levels of power have equally important contributions to the process. And if some members are not speaking or are excessively deferential, the team can talk about those dynamics and work to ensure that all team members feel comfortable expressing their opinions.

Most of our research teams have included a combination of graduate students and doctoral-level members. Some team members have had prior training or experience with research or CQR, as well as the field of psychology, and train the newer members of the team. In contrast, dissertation teams are typically led by the dissertation student, with other graduate or undergraduate students as team members and the faculty advisor as the auditor who oversees the CQR process along the way.

Another consideration is the role of the primary investigator (PI) on a CQR team. In all of the teams of which we have been a part, the PI has been a member of the research team. Power differences naturally emerge and have to be addressed if team members defer to the PI or the PI expects such deference. So, although the PI might have some additional organizational tasks (e.g., keeping track of progress on cases from interview through final audit status), the PI's role and power on the consensual team are the same as every other team member.

Configurations of Research Teams

The most common configuration is to have a set primary team of three to four members with an additional one to two auditors (more about their role later in this chapter). In this configuration, the primary team members work together on the study from start to finish, constructing the interview protocol, conducting the interviews, analyzing the data, and writing the manuscript; auditors typically provide feedback on each of these steps.

In another type of set team, one or two researchers conduct the interviews and then are joined by one or two other researchers in analyzing the data, along with one or two auditors; this method is often used in a dissertation study where the dissertator completes all the interviews. Set teams offer the advantage of allowing all primary team members to be immersed in analyzing all the data for all the cases.

Alternatively, in a rotating team structure, a larger number of team members (e.g., six to eight) rotates doing the various tasks (e.g., interviewing, domaining, developing core ideas, auditing). With rotating teams, researchers serve as primary team members on some cases (developing the domains and core ideas) and as auditors on other cases (reviewing the domains and core ideas of other teams' cases). The advantages of this strategy are that rotating teams can analyze larger data sets, and more viewpoints can be obtained. A disadvantage is that not all team members are as familiar with all the cases, and thus their contributions may be limited.

Training the Research Team About CQR

The amount of formal training depends on whether members of the team have used the method before. When one or two "trainers" (i.e., experienced CQRers) are embedded in the team, training can be more informal and can occur organically as the project proceeds (e.g., describing and illustrating domains, core ideas, and cross-analysis as the team begins each stage of data analysis). If most of the team members are new to CQR, however, we recommend thorough and preparatory training by an experienced CQR researcher. A suggested training outline is as follows:

- Each team member reads this book and exemplar empirical CQR articles (see Appendix).

- The CQR process is discussed in detail, focusing on data collection and analysis.

- Team members practice reaching consensus on domains, core ideas, and categories for domains in a cross-analysis using a small data sample from a completed study.

- The experienced trainer continues to consult with team members to help them learn the process and serves as an auditor who provides feedback along the way.

The Team Process

Working on a team can be valuable because it provides multiple viewpoints when examining the data. Working on a team can also be fun because of the collaboration with friends and colleagues on shared projects. It can also be intellectually stimulating to have other equally engaged people to talk with about ideas that emerge from the data.

We have found it helpful to begin the first meeting by stating the expectations that team members contribute equally to all discussions, are sensitive to nonverbal communication (e.g., be aware that silence may indicate disagreement or that physical signs of agitation may indicate that someone is uncomfortable with a decision), are willing to negotiate and correct problems as they arise, and that they support and respect each other (using active listening skills can be beneficial). Taking time to set ground rules and establish the scheduling of team meetings can minimize future difficulties. Establishing roles early on and clarifying authorship order and who will complete the various tasks also helps to build trust.

Group dynamics inevitably emerge in research teams. Although conflict is often viewed negatively, constructive conflict on a CQR team can foster multiple viewpoints and add depth to discussions as members are challenged to elaborate on their ideas so that others better understand them. If everyone already had the same point of view, there would be no need to bring a team together to do the work!

On a CQR research team, too much agreement is problematic. If a team member wants to get along and avoid conflict, "groupthink" may arise, where everyone goes along with an idea even with reservations about it (Janis, 1972). Highly cohesive groups are much more likely to engage in groupthink because their cohesiveness often correlates with unspoken understandings and the ability to work together with minimal explanations. Social psychologist McCauley (1989) noted that groupthink occurs when there is directive leadership, homogeneity of members' social background and ideology, and isolation of the group from outside sources of information and analysis. Encouraging the expression of dissenting opinions within the group, establishing a regular discussion of the group process, and using the objectivity of the outside monitor (i.e., auditor) all help minimize groupthink in CQR.

Groupthink may also arise given the inherent power imbalances in many CQR teams, as noted earlier (e.g., faculty and students on the same team). To mitigate such power differentials, we recommend that those with more power openly acknowledge the power differences and invite others to challenge their thoughts and interpretations of the data (and react nondefensively when they do so) and also rotate who speaks first (e.g., the faculty member does not always speak first or last). Doing so ideally provides space for those with less formal power to enter more easily into the discussions that are vital to a CQR project.

When power struggles emerge in groups, such dynamics should be discussed openly. Each person can be asked to state their feelings, with others listening and reflecting to make sure they understand. And then working honestly to resolve disagreements is important so that everyone is as comfortable as possible. If disagreements cannot be resolved, team members may have to decide whether they can continue with the research project. Scheduling regular dialogue about group dynamics and emphasizing the importance of each person's experience in the group is time well spent.

Finally, we suggest that research teams meet regularly so that everyone stays involved and remembers the cases. We have found that when teams meet infrequently or meetings are stretched out over several years, it is hard for everyone to stay motivated and immersed in the data.

AUDITORS

Using auditors is critical to the effectiveness of CQR (see Schlosser et al., 2012, for more about the philosophical foundation of auditing). Although the primary team meets regularly to discuss, debate, and ultimately arrive at consensus about the placement and meaning of data, the auditor exists outside this process of consensus and acts as a "check for the team" at distinct points throughout the analysis (Hill et al., 1997, p. 548). Auditors lend a fresh perspective and, as noted earlier, can reduce the potential impact of the primary team engaging in groupthink about the results (Hill et al., 2005, p. 196). Often, these individuals are content-area experts and/or individuals who have previous CQR experience. Auditors work intimately with the data separate from the primary team (and from one another in cases of multiple auditors) and thus provide the primary team with new perspectives.

As suggested earlier, the process of achieving consensus within the primary team is an evolutionary one, in which team members' initial understandings of the data may differ from one another in meaningful ways, and then they gradually arrive at consensus on their understanding of the data. So, too, the auditor helps the team move to a deeper comprehension of the data. Such a multiperspective approach "yields better decisions and has the potential to reduce individual biases" (Hill et al., 1997, p. 524). If the auditor suggests a subtle tweak to a domain name to be more representative of the data or identifies major portions of data that have not been adequately abstracted, this added perspective helps to maintain a rigorous, scientific process.

Some have asked us whether they could skip using auditors if resources are limited (e.g., for doctoral students). We discourage researchers from not using auditors because they provide valuable feedback about the data and their analysis. And we especially encourage doctoral students who have never done CQR before to use auditors, particularly their advisors, to make sure they are doing the project well. We have found that students really learn the method when, as auditors, we give them specific feedback about the domains, core ideas, and cross-analysis. And when we have not provided feedback quickly enough, doctoral students often flounder.

We recommend that, unless they are experienced, at least two auditors are included (we are frequently struck by how auditors pick up on different aspects of the data). The ideal auditor has content area expertise and familiarity with and openness to CQR. In our experience, it is helpful for auditors to be able and willing to work independently and be thorough, timely, and open and flexible. Auditors must also have the ability and willingness to attend to a lot of detail (e.g., the proper domain coding of a speaking turn) while simultaneously seeing how the pieces of the data analysis fit into a larger, overall conceptualization of the phenomenon under investigation. They must also be creative in seeking solutions to the inevitable data analysis challenges that arise in a study. Conversely, auditors are not helpful when they provide timid, limited, or no feedback; provide only superficial comments regarding the primary team's work; miss key details of the content being studied; or miss the "big picture" of the phenomenon being explored. Finally, it is wise for researchers to choose auditors with whom the primary team is comfortable and whom they trust and respect. Given that auditors will be providing critical feedback, it is important to have a solid relationship built on mutual trust and respect.

CONCLUSIONS

Getting started sets the foundation for everything to follow. You select a topic, review the literature, write a proposal, construct research questions, identify a population from which you will select and recruit your sample, and select a research team and auditors. Whew! Once you have done all these steps, you are ready to begin to develop your interview protocol and conduct the interviews (see the next chapter).

3 DEVELOPING THE INTERVIEW PROTOCOL

Throughout the remainder of the book, we provide examples of the steps involved in consensual qualitative research (CQR) using data from a published study on meaning in life in psychotherapy (Hill et al., 2015). We modified the examples somewhat to make them clearer for these exhibits and to preserve anonymity. We suggest that you read through this study in its entirety before proceeding. Exhibit 3.1 provides an example of an interview protocol for the meaning in life study.

The semistructured interview protocol is influenced by both the need to develop a rapport with participants (i.e., establish a research alliance) and the need to gather in-depth, consistent information across participants. Thus, participants are asked a common set of questions to gather a consistent body of data from all participants, and we also ask interviewers to use unscripted probes to facilitate the in-depth exploration of each individual's unique experiences.

Our interviews typically consist of three sections. In the opening section, interviewers inquire about emotionally neutral topics that are related broadly to the study's focus and thus "warm up" participants and build rapport. For instance, in the study on meaning in life, we first asked, "What

https://doi.org/10.1037/0000215-003
Essentials of Consensual Qualitative Research, by C. E. Hill and S. Knox

EXHIBIT 3.1. Interview Protocol for Study on Meaning in Life

Thank you for participating in this study. We want to remind you that all information is confidential. We will use code numbers rather than names in all analyses. Recordings will be erased after they are transcribed.

1. What gives you a sense of purpose or meaning in your life?
2. How does being a therapist provide meaning in life (MIL) for you?
3. How does conducting research provide MIL for you?
4. How does being an instructor or teacher provide MIL for you?
5. How do relationships contribute to your MIL?
6. How have your past experiences contributed to your MIL?
7. How has your cultural background influenced your MIL?
8. What role does spirituality or religion play in MIL?
9. How do you work with clients regarding MIL?
10. What was it like to participate in this interview?

gives you a sense of purpose or meaning in your life?" before exploring more specific questions about how therapists dealt with a specific situation in psychotherapy.

The second section of the interview protocol focuses intensely on the main topic of interest. Typically, areas germane to the topic are explored and may include the discussion of specific events as well as attitudes, beliefs, and feelings about such experiences. For example, in the meaning of life study, we asked key questions, such as "How does being a therapist provide meaning in life (MIL) for you?" "How does conducting research provide MIL for you?" and "How does being an instructor or teacher provide MIL for you?" When the research involves questions about specific events, we often explore antecedents to the event, a description of the event, participant reactions to the event, and consequences of the event.

In the final section of the protocol, participants are asked to reflect on broader issues related to the topic (e.g., advice about the topic, suggestions related to the topic). We also frequently ask participants why they chose to participate and how they felt about the interview. This final section helps participants decompress from any strong affect and allows the researchers to assess participants' emotional state. If the interview was particularly intense and participants remain quite upset, we ensure that they are safe and have someone to talk to should they want to do so.

We recommend that no more than eight to 10 open-ended, scripted questions be included for each hour-long interview to allow interviewers time to probe important areas and still maintain the consistent collection of data across participants. Asking too many questions and not following up on the questions often leads to "thin" or superficial data rather than an in-depth description of a participant's experience; too few questions can lead to a lack of consistent exploration across participants because researchers have not consistently probed the same areas.

All questions should be open ended without a specific response intended (e.g., "How did you respond to your therapist's challenge?"). Such questions facilitate clarification and exploration of attitudes, thoughts, or feelings and encourage elaboration of events without interviewees fearing judgment. These queries may be offered as questions (e.g., "What was your supervision relationship like?") or probes (e.g., "Tell me about your supervision relationship"). In contrast, closed questions (e.g., "Did the challenge make your therapist seem more human?") tend to cut off exploration and elicit one- or two-word answers. Moreover, researchers should avoid leading questions (e.g., "Wouldn't it be helpful if your therapist used challenges?") because they suggest a particular outcome and thus inappropriately narrow participants' responses.

Possible follow-up probes (e.g., "Tell me more about that") can also be listed in the protocol. Alternatively, or in addition, it can be left up to the interviewer to spontaneously generate probes based on what the interviewee says. We provide more detail on conducting the interview and probing in the next chapter.

REVISING, PILOTING, AND REVISING THE INTERVIEW PROTOCOL

After the initial protocol has been developed, we consult with experts knowledgeable about the topic area to ensure that our protocol captures the relevant data and addresses the central areas of inquiry. We may also seek feedback from individuals who have experienced the phenomenon of interest. Such persons have "lived the experience" and can offer feedback on the protocol that may not be readily apparent to the researchers.

To determine whether the interview protocol elicits the desired data, we then pilot it with at least two people who fulfill the participation criteria but are not part of the actual sample. These pilot interviews allow researchers to determine whether the questions yield data about the specific area of investigation and whether the questions flow logically. After the pilot interview, we actively solicit feedback from interviewees about any troublesome parts of the protocol (e.g., unclear wording, overlooked topic areas, abrupt flow) and then use this feedback and our reactions based on the interviews to revise the protocol. We often conduct a second round of pilot interviews to test the revised version. Such efforts have been invaluable in developing high-quality protocols.

NUMBER OF INTERVIEWERS AND INTERVIEWS

Researchers using CQR have to decide how many interviewers to use. Interviews are more likely to be consistent if one person conducts all of them; however, that interviewer's biases then permeate all the data. Alternatively, having several interviewers reduces the opportunity for a single researcher's approach or biases to adversely affect data collection, as long as interviewers consistently adhere to the prepared protocol. In addition, having several interviewers distributes the workload, potentially making researchers' involvement in the project more attractive and allowing all team members to have firsthand experience with the process. Problems can arise, however, if there is too much variability among interviewers in terms of style and depth of follow-up probes, suggesting the need for training, practice, and feedback.

Another decision involves the number of interviews per participant. If there are more than eight to 10 open-ended questions, it might be prudent to conduct two or more interviews with each participant. Multiple interviews can help the interviewer establish a relationship with the participant, enabling the latter to feel more comfortable describing emotionally evocative experiences. Moreover, participants may have further feelings and thoughts about the topic that can be explored in a second interview. A second interview also provides an opportunity for clarification of responses that were unclear during the first interview if the interviewers have listened to the first interview to prepare for subsequent interviews. Often, however, it is difficult to ask participants to give up more than 1 hour; if a second interview is not feasible, researchers have to decide on the most important questions to ask in one interview.

TRAINING INTERVIEWERS

Even when good interviewers have been selected, training is crucial to ensure consistent quality across interviewers. We thus conduct mock interviews during team meetings using the protocol. A researcher experienced in CQR models the interview process and addresses any questions that arise. Then, the novice researchers conduct mock interviews during team meetings. These role-plays allow experienced interviewers to give direct feedback to novice interviewers about their interviewing skills and for all interviewers to become comfortable with the interview protocol (and, if necessary, to unselect from the team people who are not able to conduct high-quality interviews). Finally, we have novice interviewers conduct pilot interviews, which reinforces their prior learning and offers further experience with the protocol. After data collection begins, we sometimes have the more experienced members of the research team conduct the first interviews of the study and have the novice interviewers listen to the recordings of these initial interviews, thereby allowing the novices an opportunity to hear the interview with a "real participant." In addition, we debrief after every interview that a novice researcher conducts, further helping to identify strategies for problems or difficulties that occur during the interview process.

RECORDING BIASES AND EXPECTATIONS

Biases in CQR are "personal issues that make it difficult for researchers to respond objectively to the data" (Hill et al., 1997, p. 539). Researchers might have positive or negative reactions to the data on the basis of their cultural backgrounds, values, beliefs, and direct or indirect experiences regarding the topic, all of which could influence data collection and data analyses (Hill et al., 2005). In contrast, expectations are defined as "beliefs that researchers have formed based on reading the literature and thinking about and developing the research questions" (Hill et al., 1997, p. 538). Thus, expectations reflect researchers' anticipations about participants' probable responses to interview questions.

We encourage researchers using CQR to become aware of their biases and expectations to minimize the impact on data collection and analysis. We want the data to reflect the participants' views rather than our biases and expectations. Furthermore, being aware of biases and expectations can enrich the research process by hearing many different perspectives and then speculating about where these perspectives come from. By recording biases and expectations before data collection and openly discussing them throughout the data analysis, researchers can increase their self-awareness about the topic and their reactions. In addition, including a description of biases and expectations in the manuscript allows readers to take the researchers' values into account as they read the study's findings (Fischer, 2009; Hill et al., 1997).

We ask team members to independently record their biases and expectations after the interview protocol has been finalized, but before data collection. For example, team members can ask themselves, "What are my thoughts, feelings, and experiences related to the topic?" "What are my expectations about how participants will respond to each interview question?" We then encourage team members to discuss these biases and expectations as a group so that the team members can learn about each other. Team members can then monitor their own and others' biases and expectations throughout data collection and analysis to minimize undue influence on the findings. We acknowledge that biases and expectations cannot be entirely avoided, nor indeed would we want them to be, because doing so would erase the human experience; instead, we can be curious about them and try to stay open to the data from the participants to learn something new.

One challenge that can arise during the articulation of biases and expectations is limited self-awareness (Rennie, 1996), due perhaps to minimal exposure to other ways of thinking. At other times, limited self-awareness may arise from psychological defenses, given that admitting such biases or expectations goes against one's identity or ideal self. For example, one may not want to think of oneself as holding any racial biases, so it may be difficult to admit to any such racial assumptions, which could result in biased interpretations of racially related data without one's awareness. To address limited self-awareness, research team members could seek out psychotherapy, additional training, or other opportunities to examine their biases. Team leaders can also encourage team members to learn about themselves throughout the research process and to discuss biases and expectations openly to increase self-knowledge.

Additional challenges may arise from the fear of potential professional and personal consequences of disclosing one's biases and expectations. Even if team members are aware of their biases, it can be challenging and embarrassing to report controversial biases (e.g., having a conservative political belief in a liberal academic setting) for fear of facing overt or covert criticism and judgment by other team members. Although it may be challenging at times, we encourage researchers using CQR to be as open as possible about their biases and expectations and to be nonjudgmental about other team members' beliefs. Such openness enhances research integrity (and leads to personal growth for research team members if handled well).

ATTENDING TO ETHICAL AND CULTURAL CONSIDERATIONS

Once your interview protocol is finalized, you can apply for approval for the research. For academics in the United States, this involves obtaining approval from the host university's institutional review board (IRB). Researchers from other countries or U.S. researchers not affiliated with universities have to determine local standards. All researchers are generally required by the IRBs to complete ethics training. We also highlight the need to conduct the research ethically, particularly in terms of protecting the confidentiality of participants, anonymizing data, storing the data securely (e.g., encrypting files), ensuring the right of participants to withdraw at any time, and being sensitive to cultural issues. All of these are concerns of IRBs and conscientious researchers (see also chapters by Burkard et al., 2012, and Inman et al., 2012, and the book by Cooper, 2016). Note that before you can change the interview protocol or your research procedures in any way after you start data collection, you must file an amendment with your IRB office.

CONCLUSIONS

Researchers using CQR have to spend considerable time developing and piloting their interview protocol and training interviewers to increase the likelihood that they will collect rich data. Researchers also have to reflect deeply on their biases and expectations and think about what they, as researchers, bring to the process to help them direct their attention to the data. It is very difficult to analyze data from inadequate or confusing interviews, so carefully preparing for the interview is crucial.

4 COLLECTING THE DATA

Now comes the exciting part of finding the best sample from the desired population and collecting the data. The work in the preparation phases now comes to fruition.

RECRUITING THE SAMPLE

In recruiting the sample, we must first think about how many participants we likely need to obtain consistency of results. Although consensual qualitative research (CQR) sample sizes have varied in the literature from three to 97, we generally recommend using 13 to 15 participants. This number typically provides a large enough sample to yield some consistency in results across participants, especially if the sample is relatively homogeneous in terms of their experiences.

If researchers think there is a good possibility that subgroups may emerge within the sample, a larger sample of 15 to 19 is advised because researchers can then subdivide the sample using either predetermined criteria or criteria that arise during the analyses. For example, Williams et al. (1998) divided

https://doi.org/10.1037/0000215-004
Essentials of Consensual Qualitative Research, by C. E. Hill and S. Knox

their sample of female counseling psychologists who had experienced a serendipitous event in their career path into those who had experienced the event pre-PhD and those who had experienced the event post-PhD because it became apparent during the analysis that these two groups of participants had different experiences. In a study on hostile or unasserted client anger directed at therapists, Hill et al. (2003) divided their results into those events that were resolved versus those that were unresolved because the analyses revealed that these were quite different experiences. But if there are not at least seven in a subsample, results can be unstable (i.e., unlikely to be found in another sample).

If using a large sample (> 20), other challenges may arise. If in-depth information is sought from each participant, researchers may have so much data that it is difficult to make sense of them and finish the project in a timely manner. In addition, if the sample is carefully chosen so that it is homogeneous (all have had similar experiences), at some point, saturation will occur (i.e., no new themes emerge), and thus not all 20 participants may have been necessary. In such cases, the team may elect to analyze and include in the study a random subset of 13 to 15 (or choose a smaller sample based on clear criteria) from their larger pool of 20 participants, although these decisions have to be stated in the written manuscript.

Researchers are more likely to obtain consistent results if they have a homogeneous sample. For example, if the research question is about countertransference among therapists, results might vary considerably according to therapist experience level and theoretical orientation. If researchers did not specifically select their sample on the basis of experience level and theoretical orientation and had a small sample so that they could not look at results for subsamples, they would probably end up with a lot of variant findings and thus would not be able to say much about their sample. It would be better, in this case, to select a sample of all experienced or all inexperienced therapists and all psychodynamic or all behavioral therapists and perhaps also select for other characteristics that might influence the data (e.g., gender, race, ethnicity).

When choosing the sample, researchers ideally select randomly from the population so that they are more likely to have a representative sample rather than one that is unique in a way that is not intended. For example, if a researcher only selected friends, the sample could be skewed on the basis of social class and education level. We acknowledge, however, that it is difficult to choose a completely random sample, and researchers should note this in the Limitations section of the manuscript (i.e., that a convenience sample was used and that a different sample might have produced different results).

The next step is recruiting, which can be challenging because you are asking potential interviewees for a fair amount of time, energy, and disclosure of personal feelings. In past CQR studies, the participation rate has varied from 4% in Hill et al. (1996) to 93% in Vivino et al. (2009). In their qualitative meta-analysis of data about why participants chose to participate, Hill et al. (2012) found that across all samples, the most frequent reasons were the wish to be helpful and thinking the topic was interesting or important. Reasons mentioned less often were having had experience with the topic, wanting to contribute to knowledge, liking qualitative research, being invited by a colleague, facilitating their own research, the topic not being invasive or exploitative, and wanting to experience a qualitative interview. Interestingly, when we divided the data into subsamples, graduate students more often participated because they had experienced the topic and wanted to help, whereas professionals more often participated because they were invited by a colleague and wanted to contribute to knowledge.

Researchers using CQR can think about what would motivate potential interviewees to participate. For example, recruiting therapists is often difficult because they are good with boundaries and saying no, they view their time as valuable, and they are reluctant to make themselves vulnerable if they do not trust the researchers. Clients, in contrast, are generally more amenable to participate in studies, but it is hard to find a way to contact them (a caution or consideration in using clients is that they may be more vulnerable to exploitation and less able to give truly informed consent). Introductory psychology students are easy to recruit if they earn extra credit for participating, but the topic has to appeal to them because they often have many options for extra credit. In contrast, graduate psychology students are often relatively easy to recruit, especially if other graduate students appeal to their sense of karma (i.e., paying back others who have helped you in your research or paying it forward to those who might help you or others in the future). Monetary compensation may help in some situations, especially if recruiting people who are not inherently interested in the topic. Finally, potential participants who feel strongly about the topic (e.g., in cases of abuse or illness) may be eager to participate and tell their stories both to help others and to be heard.

The participation rate can also be influenced by recruitment methods. For example, in Hill et al. (1996), when we sent a letter of invitation to therapists and asked those who were interested to respond using a self-addressed stamped envelope, only 4% responded, perhaps because it required too much time and energy to respond. In contrast, Gelso et al. (1999) reported a 13% participation rate when a letter was followed by a phone call. Vivino et al.

(2009) obtained a 93% return rate when therapists who had been nominated as being compassionate were personally invited, perhaps because they felt flattered and were compassionate people.

We suggest, then, several strategies to consider when recruiting, remembering that the strategies will differ according to the target sample:

- Send a personalized email or letter (rather than a mass communication), and then follow up with a personal email or phone call.

- Make it as easy as possible for potential participants to let you know that they agree to participate. Do not expect that they will take a lot of initiative to respond.

- Begin the invitation with a catchy first sentence (or subject line) to grab the reader's attention. Provide information about reasons for the study, the time commitment, details of involvement, and procedures for ensuring confidentiality so that potential participants can make good decisions about whether to participate.

- Do not harass potential participants. If people do not respond after two or three invitations, researchers can safely assume that the potential participants are not interested.

- For studies requiring that participants think about the topic before the interview, provide a copy of the interview protocol so that participants can prepare (e.g., therapists may have to review case notes to refresh their memory before talking with an interviewer about an experience of a hostile or angry client). In circumstances in which researchers fear that participants might prepare too much or give only socially desirable responses rather than genuine reactions (e.g., when we want to know their immediate reactions to feminism and do not want them to have a chance to formulate a politically correct response), we would not send the interview protocol ahead of time. We typically, however, are more concerned about providing participants with enough opportunity to reflect on the details of their experiences than we are about getting only socially desirable responses (which can be partially handled by asking open-ended questions and being nonjudgmental).

Importantly, our responsibility to participants does not end with recruitment. We must treat participants ethically, respect their autonomy and right to withdraw at any time, and recognize potential concerns about sharing deep thoughts and feelings with strangers. We send copies of interview transcripts so participants can correct mistakes or provide additional information.

Finally, we send the final draft of the manuscript so that participants can assure us that their identity has been concealed adequately and provide us feedback about the findings.

CONDUCTING THE INTERVIEW

Researchers have to make several decisions about how to conduct the interviews. They have to decide about conducting and recording the interviews, interviewing style, taking notes, and transcribing the interviews to have analyzable data.

When and How to Conduct the Interviews

Researchers must first decide whether to interview participants by phone, by video, or in person (i.e., face to face; Knox & Burkard, 2009) because there are trade-offs to different decisions. Phone interviews allow researchers to recruit widely because they do not have to travel to conduct the interviews. Furthermore, phone interviews provide some degree of safety and anonymity if the interviewer knows only a first name and a contact number. In contrast, in-person and video interviews offer access to nonverbal data (e.g., facial expressions, gestures) that can enrich the data (Carr & Worth, 2001; Shuy, 2003). Video interviews combine the benefits of in-person interviews (e.g., access to nonverbal data) with the advantages of phone interviews (e.g., low cost, no travel).

We have conducted the majority of our interviews by phone and have found that most participants have talked freely about powerful personal experiences (see also Hiller & DiLuzio, 2004). The reticent few may have been even less comfortable with face-to-face interviews, given that the phone provides some physical and psychological space (Sturges & Hanrahan, 2004). We note, however, that interviewers have to be verbally supportive with phone interviews, given that participants cannot see reassuring nods and smiles.

Recording the Interview

Researchers have to record (using at least audio but perhaps also video, depending on the means of interviewing) each interview to enable an accurate transcription of the interview (see the next section). We stress the importance of testing the recording equipment ahead of time to ensure that everything works and the recording is of high quality. It is disheartening to lose an interview due to faulty equipment, and it is not possible to replace the original interview. We use two recorders for each interview in case one fails during the interview or transcription process.

Interviewing Style

Consider the interviewee's perspective. They have agreed to share information about attitudes, beliefs, or important (and perhaps difficult and challenging) events in their lives. Interviewers often ask about intimate details of the interviewee's life, whereas interviewees know little about interviewers. During the interview, interviewees may feel vulnerable, sad, embarrassed, and judged (Adler & Adler, 2002), which can cause anxiety about privacy and confidentiality. Given this scenario, interviewers must nurture a research alliance with each interviewee and establish rapport, trust, and a sense of safety to ensure the richness and validity of the data (Adler & Adler, 2002; Knox & Burkard, 2009; Kvale, 1996; Thomas & Pollio, 2002).

Interviewers must also balance providing support with obtaining the desired data for the study. To achieve this balance, interviewers use empathy to help participants feel safe and develop enough trust so that the interviewer may fully but gently probe participants' experiences. In these interviews, interviewers use the protocol's open-ended questions to ask about the experiences and then restate and reflect feelings to make sure they understand what the participant has said (for more description of these skills, see Hill, 2020). Importantly, however, interviewers should avoid giving too much praise or reassurance because it could unduly influence the interview and make the interviewees feel that they need to please the interviewer.

In addition, interviewers must maintain a sense of curiosity and not be judgmental because participants are likely to shut down if they feel that the interviewer is evaluating them. Interviewers also have to be aware of their reactions to participant disclosures, given that interviewees often "read" interviewers' reactions to disclosures and alter what they share (Marcus & Crane, 1986; Musselwhite et al., 2007). Furthermore, interviewers generally offer minimal self-disclosure so as not to bias participant responses and divert the focus of the interview from the participant to the researcher. Of course, it would not be possible (or desirable) for interviewers to remain neutral during the interview process, because such neutrality could result in a sterile, uncompassionate tone.

Inevitably, interviewers will face difficulties during the interview, so it is good to be prepared for such eventualities. For example, some participants do not disclose enough information and thus may need additional probing to elicit the desired data. Other participants may experience intense emotions during the interview. Although such participants are usually able to continue if given support and reassurance, they may need a short break to allow them to refocus in the interview. If it seems appropriate, interviewers might ask participants whether there is something about the interview content or relationship that is causing their discomfort and then change their approach to meet the interviewee's needs. When participants' responses are vague, unclear, or tangential, we return to questions that were not directly answered and try to rephrase them in a new way so that participants can better respond. On occasion, we also might gently interrupt participants who go off on tangents and refocus them to get the desired information.

When participants try to control the interview by asking and then answering the questions (especially if they have reviewed the interview protocol before the interview), the interviewer gently interrupts and reminds the participant that the interviewer has to ask the questions. Finally, when participants ask for interviewer disclosure about the topic, we often briefly disclose a shared experience or belief and then turn the focus back to the interviewee by asking how the interviewee felt, thereby ensuring that the interview remains focused on the participant.

As noted in the previous chapter, probes are used to help participants explore their individual experiences more deeply and richly. For instance, after participants have shared an experience, we might probe for their unique attitudes or emotions related to the events, how they behaved in such situations, what they were thinking during the event, or what they noticed about others' reactions to help participants more fully describe their experiences. To probe participants' responses more deeply, we encourage researchers to be keenly attuned not only to the content of what is said but also how it is said (e.g., tone of voice, pauses, change in volume), both of which may yield additional rich data.

Finally, interviewees may occasionally hint at but not explicitly verbalize their thoughts or feelings. In such circumstances, interviewers might offer a tentative interpretation or explanation to help interviewees describe their experience more explicitly. If, however, interviewees respond only passively (e.g., saying "Mm-hmm" without elaboration) to such interviewer statements, we cannot later determine whether they actually agreed with the interviewer. Thus, interviewers have to ask the interviewees to state their thoughts overtly so that we have their own words about what they are thinking and feeling. Note that the goal is to help interviewees more clearly state their thoughts rather than introducing new explanations for interviewees to consider.

Taking Notes During and After Interviews

We recommend that researchers take notes during the interview to help them stay actively involved, remind themselves about additional questions they might want to ask, and provide information in case the tapes are hard to hear during transcription. In addition, we urge researchers to write about their experience of the interview at its conclusion (e.g., recording whether there was rapport with participants, how detailed and rich the participants' responses were, reactions evoked in the researcher by participants or their responses) to remind themselves of what it was like to be with this interviewee. Such data can later provide context for puzzling or vague interview content. For example, in one study, an interviewer noted some possible fragility or overwhelming emotions in the interviewee about the topic, which later helped the research team better conceptualize the interviewee's experience.

Transcribing

Because transcribing is crucial for putting the interview data into a form that can be analyzed, we provide transcribers with clear instructions. For example, we ask transcribers to use *I* for interviewer and *P* for participant and ask them to number the speaking turns in the transcript (e.g., the interviewer's first speaking turn would be labeled I1, the participant's first speaking turn P1, the interviewer's second speaking turn I2, the participant's second speaking turn P2, and so forth). Some researchers also add line numbers to the transcript so that they can later locate the quotes. Transcribers de-identify names, cities, states, countries, businesses, or universities; transcribe all utterances verbatim; and indicate nonverbal data such as pauses, sighs, laughter, or crying in parentheses. Transcribers may be required to complete ethics training, certainly must maintain confidentiality, and must store recordings in a secure location. Once completed, a second person reviews the transcript by listening to the audiotape and examining the transcript for accuracy, completeness, and confidentiality. When the transcript is complete, the recording is deleted (unless needed for the data analysis, after which it is deleted). New web services are now available for creating transcripts relatively inexpensively, but our experience is that transcripts still have to be checked carefully for accuracy by listening to the recording of the interview.

CONCLUSIONS

Recruiting a good sample is crucial for obtaining clear and interpretable data, so considerable attention has to be given to thoughtfully choosing the sample and then recruiting specific participants. Furthermore, careful attention must also be given to the interview process and transcribing interviews. Without good data, researchers will not be able to engage in good data analyses and will have difficulty interpreting the results.

5 ANALYZING DATA WITHIN CASES

In this chapter, we describe the data analysis within cases. We first develop domains that reflect the topic areas of the interview data. We then construct core ideas from the domained data in each case.

DOMAINS

We think of domains as broad subject areas (i.e., topics interviewees talk about). Later, during the cross-analysis, we identify themes within domains. For example, a domain might be "experience of the interview," whereas, in the cross-analysis, we might identify themes such as "pleasant," "uncomfortable," and "informative" to reflect the data within that domain. Thus, with the domains, we are not describing what we found, but rather identifying the broad areas into which our data fit. The domains are thus a tool for organizing our data.

Developing the Domain List

A domain list reflects the meaningful and distinct topic areas covered in the interview. We typically develop a domain list by reading through one

https://doi.org/10.1037/0000215-005
Essentials of Consensual Qualitative Research, by C. E. Hill and S. Knox

transcript together as a team and proposing ideas for potential domains. We suggest no more than 10 to 15 domains (although you later may develop sub-domains). Next, we apply this preliminary domain list to another transcript and modify it as needed to fit that transcript, given that domains may have to be added, deleted, or otherwise altered. We continue this process with new transcripts until no more domains emerge. The list thus begins to stabilize as the team gains a deeper understanding of the interviews and as the content of the data becomes clearer. This process requires considerable debate because team members typically focus on different levels of complexity of the data. We want the domains to be neither too large and global (e.g., a domain of all therapy events) nor too tiny and specific (e.g., a domain called "when clients laugh because something strikes them as silly" is too specific, whereas a domain called "when clients laugh" is a more helpful way to capture such content) because both make it difficult to organize the data effectively.

An alternate method for developing domains, which applies mostly to experienced teams, is to have all team members independently read three to four transcripts and develop possible domains that can be discussed and argued through until they construct a consensus list. They then apply this list to two to three new transcripts, revising as necessary until a stable list is obtained.

Note that the domains do not necessarily match the questions on the interview protocol, although there is typically some overlap, given that the same questions are asked of everyone. In fact, while developing the domains, team members would do well to *not* go back to the interview questions but rather to rely on the data that emerge from the interviews, given that new and unexpected domains might arise that may not have been focused on in the interview protocol.

At this point, then, researchers have a tentative domain list (further changes will undoubtedly be necessary throughout the analysis to refine the list as our understanding of the data increases). We then put these proposed domains in a logical order (e.g., if the study focused on participants' experience of a particular event, we would likely identify a domain of "event antecedents," followed by "the event itself," and then followed by "event consequences"). We include an "Other" domain at the end as a place for parts of interviews that do not fit elsewhere or are not relevant. We assign a number to each domain (the number itself has no meaning, but it assists researchers in working with the data as the analysis process continues).

We then ask the auditor(s) to review the domain list. They provide feedback about the clarity of the domain titles, the level of specificity of the domains (e.g., too vague, broad, or too narrow), overlap between domains, and ordering of the domains. See Exhibit 5.1 for the domain list constructed for the meaning in life study mentioned in Chapter 3.

Coding the Interview Data Into the Domains

Once the domain list is established, we mark each chunk or block of data (i.e., phrases, thought units, sentences, or paragraphs that cover the same topic area) as belonging to at least one of the domains. Occasionally, we might double- or triple-code some data if they fit into more than one domain. When researchers find themselves double- and triple-coding a substantial portion of the data, this is often an indication that domains have to be combined or modified.

We usually do the domaining work as a team. After reading a chunk of data out loud until the topic changes, each team member independently writes down the domain to which the data belong. Then we rotate who speaks first about which domain is most appropriate, stating rationales for opinions until all have spoken. We discuss all differences of opinion and come to a consensus regarding the domains that are the best fit for the data.

There will likely be some data in each transcript that are irrelevant to the focus of the study (e.g., greetings, scheduling, reviewing the informed consent, interruptions) and thus will not be included in the data analysis. Because these data will not be coded, researchers can consensually agree to eliminate them from the consensus version of the case (defined later). Likewise, some data might seem relevant to the study but do not fit comfortably

---

EXHIBIT 5.1. Domain List for Study on Meaning in Life (MIL)

1. Being a therapist as a source of MIL
2. Conducting research as a source of MIL
3. Being a teacher as a source of MIL
4. Professional activities other than therapy, research, teaching that provide MIL
5. Religion or spirituality as a source of MIL
6. Relationships as a source of MIL
7. Personal or nonprofessional activities that are sources of MIL
8. Influence of culture on MIL
9. Influence of past experiences on MIL
10. Influence of money on MIL
11. Influence of control (internal, external, destiny, calling) on MIL
12. Working with clients about MIL
13. Experience of interview
14. Other

into any of the constructed domains. We put these data into the "Other" domain (as noted earlier) so that we can go back later and determine whether there is enough consistency across cases within the "Other" domain to identify a new domain.

Once the team has worked together to assign interview data to domains in four to six transcripts, they are usually becoming consistent and competent in their ability to complete this domaining task. If new domains are not emerging and all team members feel confident about the domaining process, we sometimes assign two team members (usually including the interviewer of the case) to work together to "domain" the remaining transcripts. We rotate the teams so that team members get exposure to different ways of thinking. Other team members then review the cases and act as "internal" auditors so that all team members have been exposed to all interview data. Any disagreements in domaining are discussed until consensus is reached. Transcripts used to develop the initial domain list are re-domained at the end of the domaining process.

Exhibit 5.2 provides an exercise for readers to domain a small section of an interview, using the domain list provided in Exhibit 5.1. Circle each block or chunk of data, and in the margin, indicate to which domain(s) it belongs. Once you have completed this exercise, go to Exhibit 5.3 and see how our team assigned domains to these data.

Consensus Version

We now create a consensus version (CV) for each case (i.e., a new document that includes all the raw data placed into domains). Exhibit 5.4 shows how this CV would look for one domain: The domain name is listed at the top, followed by a chunk of raw data, and a place to write the core ideas (see the next section). We have used other formats (e.g., Excel, tables) but cannot show them all here because of space considerations. Each team can use whatever format works best for them as long as the auditors can easily review the data.

When copying the data from the transcript to the consensus version, include what the interviewer said so that those analyzing the data can understand interviewees' responses in the context of the interviewer's questions or statements. Of additional importance is that interviewees have to have actually said in the interview what then is coded into the domain (i.e., the chunk cannot rely solely on what the researcher says because it might not be an accurate representation of the interviewee's viewpoint).

EXHIBIT 5.2. Developing Domains Exercise

Instructions: Circle or bracket the interview data that reflect the domains shown in Exhibit 5.1. Use the number assigned to each domain to identify which data fit in which domain(s).

I12: So, what gives you a sense of purpose or meaning in life?

P12: My work and relationships are the two very strong things. When I'm feeling good about those two things, I can be with myself, and that to me shows me that I'm in a good place—just being myself and being happy. Do you want me to get into specifics?

I13: Yeah [both laugh].

P13: . . . The first thing that almost came into my mind was therapy, so clinical work, and it gives me a lot of meaning in terms of [silence] it just I don't even know . . . I'm worried about making it too much about me being with the client . . . being in that moment with someone and sharing that gives me a lot of [silence] it just, it makes me feel good . . . if I can just be with that person, if I can help in any way, it gives me a lot of meaning. I remember when I first realized that it just felt like such an instant connection, it just felt that this was what I was meant to do. I remember when I first started work with kids, and then it moved on to families, and then I think right now in the program, it's at a completely different level of, I mean, I think I explored a lot of options, and I came here, and now it just sometimes feels like this was my purpose, you know, in terms of listening, it feels like it comes naturally to me. I don't struggle; it affects me in a very deep way, but even if I'm really, really sad about something about a client, there's a sense of peace . . . I thought about research [laughs], and I'm not sure, you know. I realized this this past week that I don't know if I haven't found that kind of meaning yet with research that with clinical work I think I get instantly. I don't know if I'll have to look at it more. I think I enjoy research. Like, I feel excited, there are a lot of parts. I'm presenting at a conference; this presentation gives me a huge sense of excitement. I love listening to research, but I hesitate calling it my life's purpose. It doesn't give me that same sort of feeling. It gives me a sense of excitement, of accomplishment, so [silence].

I14: So, you kind of feel more of a connection to, like, conducting therapy than conducting research, and though you really enjoy both of them you [silence].

P14: Yeah, the therapy connection seems deeper. I think research I enjoy, but the parts of research I enjoy are connected to therapy. That's what's guiding my research. My research is on therapy and on the therapy relationship, so I imagine that it will grow. Research is relatively new for me, whereas therapy and this helping sort of role has been around for many years. I have a feeling that this research thing will grow.

Note. I = interviewer; P = participant or interviewee.

EXHIBIT 5.3. Example of Domained Raw Data

Domain 1: Being a Therapist as a Source of Meaning in Life

I12:   So, what gives you a sense of purpose or meaning in life?

P12:   My work and relationships are two very strong things. When I'm feeling good about those two things, I can be with myself, and that to me shows me that I'm in a good place—just being myself and being happy. Do you want me to get into specifics?

I13:   Yeah [both laugh].

P13:   . . . The first thing that almost came into my mind was therapy, so clinical work, and it gives me a lot of meaning in terms of [silence] it just I don't even know . . . I'm worried about making it too much about me being with the client . . . being in that moment with someone and sharing that gives me a lot of [silence] it just, it makes me feel good . . . if I can just be with that person, if I can help in any way, it gives me a lot of meaning. I remember when I first realized that it just felt like such an instant connection, it just felt that this was what I was meant to do. I remember when I first started work with kids, and then it moved on to families, and then I think right now in the program, it's at a completely different level of, I mean, I think I explored a lot of options, and I came here, and now it just sometimes feels like this was my purpose, you know, in terms of listening, it feels like it comes naturally to me. I don't struggle; it affects me in a very deep way, but even if I'm really, really sad about something about a client, there's a sense of peace.

I14:   So, you kind of feel more of a connection to, like, conducting therapy than conducting research, and though you really enjoy both of them you [silence].

P14:   Yeah, the therapy connection seems deeper.

Domain 2: Conducting Research as a Source of Meaning in Life

P13:   . . . I thought about research [laughs], and I'm not sure, you know. I realized this this past week that I don't know if I haven't found that kind of meaning yet with research that with clinical work I think I get instantly. I don't know if I'll have to look at it more. I think I enjoy research. Like, I feel excited, there are a lot of parts. I'm presenting at a conference; this presentation gives me a huge sense of excitement. I love listening to research, but I hesitate calling it my life's purpose. It doesn't give me that same sort of feeling. It gives me a sense of excitement, of accomplishment, so [silence].

P14:   . . . I think research I enjoy, but the parts of research I enjoy are connected to therapy. That's what's guiding my research. My research is on therapy and on the therapy relationship, so I imagine that it will grow. Research is relatively new for me, whereas therapy and this helping sort of role has been around for many years. I have a feeling that this research thing will grow.

Domain 6: Relationships as a Source of Meaning in Life

I12:   So, what gives you a sense of purpose or meaning in life?

P12:   My work and relationships are the two very strong things. When I'm feeling good about those two things, I can be with myself, and that to me shows me that I'm in a good place—just being myself and being happy.

Note. I = interviewer; P = participant or interviewee.

We note that we do all the copying of data from the interview transcript to the CV ourselves using word processing programs rather than using any commercial software packages for qualitative data. We have not found an inexpensive program that fits our needs and do not find it that difficult to do the task ourselves. What is most important for later steps of the analysis is that all units or chunks of data are assigned to at least one domain, that the domain and raw data are placed next to each other in the CV, and that the line or speaking turn numbers from the original transcribed version of the text are maintained in the consensus version to facilitate later checking of the raw data.

We send the CV of the first two cases to the auditor(s) to check the domaining process. If the auditor has major concerns, we go back and rethink the domains. Once the auditor has "approved" the domaining, we wait to send more CVs to the auditor(s) until we have included the core ideas so that the auditor(s) can review the domains and core ideas together.

CORE IDEAS

Core ideas are summaries that capture the essence of the interviewee's statements in fewer and often clearer words. Constructing core ideas involves paraphrasing the narrative, thus transforming the interview data into clear, understandable, and consistent language so that researchers can compare core ideas across cases. Constructing core ideas is necessary because participants often are confusing or contradictory, ramble, repeat themselves, and use shorthand to refer back to what they said previously. Their statements are often unclear when taken out of context, so we try to make core ideas clear and precise to reflect what the participant has said. In addition, we try to remain close to the data while constructing core ideas (i.e., using participants' words if possible).

We suggest that research team members read through the data in each domain before the meeting to familiarize themselves with the case. Research team members then work together to construct core ideas during the meeting. We have team members rotate reading the relevant interview data out loud and offering core ideas. Other team members provide feedback on the proposed core ideas and thus help each other avoid making assumptions, inferring intentions, or using psychological jargon. By talking about their understanding of the data within the context of the case, team members separate their beliefs and biases from what the participant is actually saying.

EXHIBIT 5.4. Developing Core Ideas Exercise for One Interviewee for Domain 1: "Being a Therapist as a Source of Meaning in Life"

Instructions: Generate core ideas for this section of data for the domain, "Being a therapist as a source of meaning in life." Develop core ideas only for the data that are relevant to this specific domain (i.e., if some data appear but are not related to this specific domain, do not core them here).

P13: I mean I was thinking about that too when C said meaning of life, and I really thought it was interesting, but the first thing that almost came into my mind was therapy, so clinical work, and it gives me a lot of meaning in terms of [silence] it just I don't even know. I don't want to take away. I don't know how to put this. I'm worried about making it too much about me being with the client, but I think, yeah, all things considered, being in that moment with someone and sharing that gives me a lot of [silence] it just, it makes me feel good. It makes me feel, if I can just be with that person, if I can help in any way, it gives me a lot of meaning. It feels, I mean, I remember when I first realized that it just felt like such an instant connection, it just felt that this was what I was meant to do. I remember when I first started work with kids, and then it moved on to families, and then I think right now in the program it's at a completely different level of, I think I explored a lot of options, and I came here, and now it just sometimes feels like this was my purpose, you know, in terms of listening, it feels like it comes naturally to me. I don't struggle; it affects me in a very deep way, but even if I'm really, really sad about something about a client, there's a sense of peace. So, I think clinical work is huge.

I14: So, you kind of feel more of a connection to, like, conducting therapy than conducting research, and though you really enjoy both of them you [silence]

P14: Yeah, the therapy connection seems deeper.

[Place core ideas here.]

I39: You mentioned a lot about being a therapist and how that gives you meaning, but could you go over it more in detail, about how being a therapist provides meaning in life for you?

P40: I'm trying not to think about the bad sessions and about the good sessions so that I walk away with that feeling. I don't know, it's really hard to explain [silence]. Well, I guess, a couple of things. The first thing is that connection. That's why I really like the therapy relationship because I just feel like just forming that connection is so meaningful. There's someone you can just sit with and talk to, and I can give that space, and someone can learn something from themselves, and that for me is so meaningful. I'm part of that, you know. I'm part of that experience. It's hugely so much satisfying. I still remember moments where my client has learned something about themselves, or I remember the sort of emotional connection and emotional insight, and it shows in that second, I felt [silence] a sense of being satisfied. Like being moved. I think I felt more moved than being satisfied. Yeah, I just felt so moved, like I'm part of this, I'm part of this experience with this person and, in this second, they've shown me something they haven't shown anyone or made this connection they've not shared with anyone. And I felt really hopeful that this would help the person too, like. So, I think sharing that with that person is so meaningful to me. I may feel

EXHIBIT 5.4. Developing Core Ideas Exercise for One Interviewee for Domain 1: "Being a Therapist as a Source of Meaning in Life" *(Continued)*

uncomfortable, and that's why I struggle with therapy too because I'm saying I'm helping the person or that I'm doing something. Like, I think that's what I was trying to say when I first talked about this therapy thing. I don't want to take ownership, like I almost felt like the client or the person has reached self-understanding but has shared it with me, or my presence has facilitated that self-understanding, but I don't like roles where guiding them, that sort of notion, but I think that sharing is very meaningful to me. The other thing that's very meaningful is that sense of curiosity and understanding, and I'm just like, you know, just sort of linking what is making a person who they are, and I've always looked at my past, you know, how my past experiences have shaped who I am and sort of looking at it more intellectually from a more theoretical perspective. I think I've always, always have had this sense of wonder that there's something there like, wow, it blows me away, you know? And I think that gives me meaning, like I think it's, yeah. Yeah, it's like this feeling of wonder, like how, like something that's happened so many years ago, this is what's happening, this is what makes sense . . . yeah, and just sort of valuing how much, how experiences can change people or having impact on people, and people don't sort of realize, or how people can contribute to so many individual differences in people. So, all of that really sort of helps keep you, like, derive meaning from that.

[Place core ideas here.]

I41: So, it's kind of that really, really strong sense of curiosity and discovery about the client's lives and trying to figure out the best way to help them but not wanting to take credit for it and wanting them to become independent.

P41: Yeah, and I like that therapy is always so challenging, and I think that's what doesn't make it boring for me. It makes me feel things that I haven't prepared for. I always feel with my clients when they leave that I've learned something, so I think it adds so much to my personal goals. Like, I learn a lot from my clients, so I think that's another piece too. I think every client I have seen has taught me something about myself or taught me something in some way. Like, I think there are lessons I have learned, whether it's connecting the feelings they're having that I haven't had or I can identify that feeling better. If they see me in a certain way, like, I always wonder is there a part of myself that is, like, that that I'm not aware of? As I see clients, I mean, I just sort of realized, for example, I hadn't realized how much anger is an issue for me. Cause I deal with anger fine in very close interpersonal relationships. I express anger, I can typically take anger, but with certain figures it's really hard for me to take anger, and I remember the first time this came out was through my work with a client, and I never realized that about myself, so it's also like a discovery about them, but it's also discovering so much about myself, so it feels like while I'm sharing this experience with them I'm growing too, and I think that's very meaningful.

[Place core ideas here.]

Note. C = client; I = interviewer; P = participant or interviewee.

Team members sometimes differ about the level of detail to include in the core ideas. For example, one team member might think it is important to state that "the session ran over by 14 minutes because the client did not want to leave because she had more to say," whereas another might just say "the session ran overtime." This decision depends on the centrality of the domain for the focus of the study, such that more central domains warrant greater specificity in the core ideas because such details often prove to be important in the analyses for understanding the data. The team must come to a consensus about how much detail is necessary.

As a guideline, we suggest that the core ideas should be briefer than the raw data and include only the essential, nontrivial details. We also suggest keeping focused on the intent of the specific domain, making sure that data are cored in response to the topic of the domain. Thus, in the case of double-domained data, the core ideas will vary according to the intent of the specific domain (e.g., different core ideas may be needed if the participant talked about both reactions to the therapist [one domain] and reactions to a partner [a different domain] in the same speaking turn). When disagreements occur while constructing the core ideas, researchers go back to the interview data to check what was said.

It is helpful if the person responsible for the CV records the core ideas directly into the CV in the computer and displays the core ideas onto an overhead projector (or on a shared screen across computers) so that everyone can see and comment on the cores as they are being constructed. Core ideas can also be written longhand and transferred later into the CV if technology is not available.

We find it helpful to replace pronouns in the data with agreed-on designations (e.g., "he," "she," or "they" become "P" for participant, "C" for client, "T" for therapist) to protect confidentiality and remove potential biases related to gender. If gender is of interest, researchers could compare subsamples later (unless, of course, knowing the gender is key to understanding the context of the case). The team might also create a title for each case (e.g., "The Sausage Eater") to remind themselves of the key features of the case.

Once the team has cored several transcripts together and everyone feels confident in creating core ideas, the team may elect to alter their process to make it more efficient. For example, rotating teams of two judges each could work together to develop the core ideas for an entire case, with other team members reviewing those cores (acting as internal auditors) so that all team members stay close to the data.

An exercise for constructing core ideas is presented in Exhibit 5.4. Examples of how our team constructed the core ideas are shown in Exhibit 5.5.

EXHIBIT 5.5. Example of Core Ideas for One Interviewee for Domain 1: "Being a Therapist as a Source of Meaning in Life"

Core ideas for PK I13–P14:

- When asked about meaning in life, P first thought of therapy.
- P feels like P was meant to do therapy.
- Doing therapy comes naturally to P and affects P in a deep way.
- P feels a sense of peace and feels good when doing therapy.
- P feels connection with clients when doing therapy.

Core ideas for PK I39–P41:

- It is meaningful to have a connection and be part of the experience of giving space for a person to learn about themselves, which makes P feel satisfied and moved because P is part of something, a connection C has not shared with anyone.
- P is hopeful such connections would help C.
- P is a bit uncomfortable because P does not want to take ownership of C's self-understanding.
- Rather, C has reached self-understanding and has shared that with P, or P's presence has facilitated but not guided C's self-understanding, which is meaningful.
- Curiosity and understanding are also meaningful because links what is making C who C is.
- P feels wonder that something that occurred years ago continues to have an influence. P values how much experiences can change or affect people even if people do not realize it.
- Psychotherapy is not boring because it is challenging and makes P feel things P is not prepared for.
- When Cs learn something, it also adds to P's personal goals, and P learns from Cs.
- If Cs see P in certain way, P wonders whether there is a part of P that P is not aware of (e.g., P has realized how much anger is an issue for P).
- Psychotherapy is discovery and growth for both C and P, which is meaningful.

Note. PK = participant code; I = interviewer; P = participant or interviewee; C = client. Raw data that served as the basis for the core ideas are shown in Exhibit 5.4.

AUDIT

The CV of each case, with the domains and core ideas indicated, is sent for review to the auditors, who try to be as detailed as possible in providing feedback so that the team can profit from an outside perspective. As described earlier, auditors play an essential role in the quality and trustworthiness of CQR. Like a good editor, they attend to small details as well as to the big picture. Like a good consultant, they affirm and expand on the primary team's findings. They disagree with and challenge the primary team to think about the data in new ways and provide the primary team with a useful system of checks and balances.

When two auditors are used, the data can either be sent to both auditors at the same time or sent first to one and then to the other after the feedback from the first is addressed. In the latter case, the team essentially receives a completely new audit after the initial revisions have been made based on the first audit. As noted before, we are often surprised at how different the feedback is across auditors, supporting the value of having more than one auditor.

Auditors immerse themselves in the data of each case. They review the raw data, read the core ideas developed by the primary team, and determine whether anything is missing and whether the core ideas could be improved. They assess whether the core ideas are crisp, concise, well-articulated, nonredundant, appropriate for the domain, and close to the words of the participants. They also review the domain titles to determine whether these adequately reflect the interview data.

Auditor feedback is generally presented in writing (rather than in person). The auditor might provide comments directly on the document using something like Track Changes, summarize the changes in an email noting the page and line numbers, or write the comments on a hard copy of the document.

The Feedback Loop

Once the auditors review the CV, the team meets to discuss the feedback and decide whether to make the recommended changes. In the case of disagreements within the team or between the team and the auditor, the primary team goes back to the transcript or to the recorded interview to resolve conflicts. Several iterations between the auditor(s) and team are sometimes needed, especially at the beginning of the process, until everyone agrees that the core ideas are clear and adequately represent the data.

The primary team has a right to disagree with and ultimately disregard auditors' comments if they have sound reasons for doing so and come to a consensus after much consideration (except in the situation of a master's thesis or doctoral dissertation; see the next paragraph). In practice, most primary teams accept some of the auditor's recommendations and reject others through a cyclical feedback process. If there is considerable disagreement between the team and an auditor, they might have to reconsider their process. As noted by Hill et al. (1997),

> If the team is ignoring everything the auditor says or the auditor makes no suggestions, there is some basis for concern about the process. In such cases, the team might need to meet with the auditor to resolve disagreements or misunderstandings and clarify thinking. (pp. 548–549)

The primary team's dialogue about a decision to ignore a recommendation made by the auditor should be thorough and thoughtful, and their rationale should be clear and compelling.

Somewhat different guidelines apply to students using CQR for a master's thesis or doctoral dissertation. We suggest that the advisor, who is usually an auditor, be involved at all stages of the process in guiding the student and preventing unnecessary missteps. Hence, the advisor asks the team leader for evidence about how the team is functioning and how they process the audits and intervenes when disputes arise. Such close contact with the primary team is beneficial for preventing major problems, especially when the team is learning the process.

Negotiating Relationships Between the Primary Team and Auditors

As noted earlier, problems sometimes arise between the primary team and auditors. The primary team might feel that the auditor is dismissing their hard work and is not "getting it." In contrast, the auditor may struggle with the idea that the primary team has the "final say" regarding the incorporation of feedback. If the primary team or auditor continues to feel strongly about an idea, we suggest a further dialogue between the primary team and the auditor(s). A phone or face-to-face meeting may help resolve differences.

Before requesting this dialogue, all parties involved should spend time considering their reactions. If there is a legitimate concern that the primary team or auditor has dismissed something inappropriately (e.g., due to biases that they may hold, one member of the primary team being domineering, the perceived impact of groupthink), this meeting is warranted. If the reaction comes, however, from a more personal place (e.g., the auditor has difficulty with rejection, primary team members are having difficulty filtering out their biases in analyzing the data), they should seek to resolve what may be negatively affecting their participation in the data analysis before requesting such a meeting. An advantage of working with seasoned CQR researchers as auditors is that they will have had the experience of accepting and rejecting another auditor's feedback when serving as a member of a primary team. Recalling this experience can help auditors take the current team's decisions less personally.

CONCLUSIONS

Parsing the interview data into domains and constructing core ideas requires considerable attention to the context of the case, judgment, care, and openness to each team member's thoughts. We want to ensure that the data analysis reflects the participants rather than ourselves. Multiple perspectives hopefully yield different viewpoints that help us arrive at a good construction of the data.

6 ANALYZING DATA ACROSS CASES

The cross-analysis involves identifying common themes (categories) within domains across cases (we use the terms *themes* and *categories* synonymously). The cross-analysis yields the findings that most of us think of when we talk about the results of a project (e.g., a description of the types of experiences clients had when they felt misunderstood in therapy, a description of the different ways parents responded when children had tantrums).

THE CROSS-ANALYSIS

To prepare for the cross-analysis, researchers compile the core ideas for each domain from all cases into one mega-document (which we sometimes affectionately refer to as the "beast"). Researchers now no longer work directly with the raw transcript text (unless problems arise) and instead work with the core ideas to identify themes. Researchers do, however, retain the case number and speaking turn numbers (or line numbers) associated with each core idea to enable them to go back to the original transcript as needed to clarify or resolve disagreements.

https://doi.org/10.1037/0000215-006
Essentials of Consensual Qualitative Research, by C. E. Hill and S. Knox

Researchers conduct the cross-analysis one domain at a time. We suggest starting with a relatively small and easy domain so that the team can gain competence with the task.

Developing Categories

Throughout the process of domaining and coring, the team members likely have had initial thoughts about possible themes, and now is the time for them to see how the data fit together. Team members together review all the core ideas within a given domain and identify common themes across cases. The goal here is to create a category structure that best captures the data within the domain.

We typically rotate reading the core ideas out loud and proposing ideas about themes or patterns that emerge from the cores. As we continue reading, we may further refine the evolving categories into subcategories (e.g., subtypes of positive experiences with therapist self-disclosure; see Exhibit 6.1 for examples of subcategories within categories). We work toward a consensus regarding which categories to include and what to label these categories. We derive category titles from the data rather than from preconceived notions about the categories. Alternatively, team members (especially if they are researchers experienced with consensual qualitative research [CQR]) independently review the data ahead of time and come prepared with possible categories and subcategories that can be discussed and negotiated.

Some domains could have relatively few categories, whereas others could have several categories, depending on the nature and amount of data (i.e., cores) in the domain. In addition, subcategories are common within larger domains to more clearly describe the findings.

The process of creating categories is hopefully lively and creative because the analysis is now out of the "trees" of domaining and coring and finally

EXHIBIT 6.1. Example of Cross-Analysis Categories and Subcategories for Domain 1: "Being a Therapist as a Source of Meaning in Life"

1. Being a therapist as a source of meaning in life
   1.a. Self-oriented meanings from being a therapist
      1.a.i. Feels fulfilled and efficacious
      1.a.ii. Provides personal growth and insight
      1.a.iii. Allows for connection and intimacy
      1.a.iv. Fulfills a talent
   1.b. Other-oriented meanings from being a therapist
      1.b.i. Helps others
      1.b.ii. Makes the world a better place

into the "forest" of the emerging themes or patterns. This level of creating categories can be done most effectively by judges who have immersed themselves in the cases and know the data well. Exhibit 6.1 shows the categories and subcategories developed for the meaning in life study for the section of the data related to being a therapist as a source of meaning.

Placing the Core Ideas Into Categories

Now that the tentative categories for a domain have been generated, each discrete core idea for each participant is placed within one or more categories or subcategories. Note that often the core ideas have to be divided at this point so that only the relevant portions are placed in the appropriate category or subcategory (i.e., a core may contain content relevant to more than one category; only the content that fits the specific category is placed in that category). We do this step by having team members rotate reading the core ideas out loud and suggesting which category is most appropriate, with the team then consensually deciding into which category (or categories) the core idea should be placed.

The initial category list evolves as the team places the core ideas into categories. Some changes are relatively minor, such as changing the title of a category. Other changes are more major, such as redefining the categories themselves, increasing or decreasing the number of categories or subcategories, or collapsing or expanding some categories. When, in the process of categorizing the core ideas, researchers notice that a core idea is unclear, they return to the raw data and consensually modify the core idea, following each modification with appropriate corrections to the consensus version of the case and to the "beast."

Although researchers try to develop categories and subcategories that capture all the data, a few core ideas inevitably will not fit into any meaningful category or subcategory. Core ideas that reflect unique experiences reported by only one participant, tangents in the data that are not relevant to the study, or core ideas that defy categorization are placed in an "Other" category. At the end of the cross-analyses, the team examines the core ideas in "Other" categories to see whether they can fit into existing categories or whether new categories can be developed.

Exhibit 6.2 provides an exercise for learning about cross-analyses: Readers can take the core ideas from two cases and place them in the categories and subcategories shown in Exhibit 6.1 for Domain 1 (Being a Therapist as a Source of Meaning). Exhibit 6.3 then shows how our team placed the core ideas from these two cases into the cross-analysis categories.

EXHIBIT 6.2. Cross-Analysis Exercise for "Being a Therapist as a Source of Meaning in Life"

Instructions: Develop themes or categories that emerge from the core ideas below. These themes or categories should include data from at least two cases. Cases have been deidentified by using the interviewer's initials and speaking turn numbers from the transcript.

VB I3-P15: P tries to not only listen to P's clients but also the subtext, emotion, and the way things are said. P derives lots of meaning from sessions because P can see how giving to someone in the moment impacts them.

VB P11: P believes that completely immersing herself with a client gives P meaning in life.

VB I13-P13: P finds being a therapist the most meaningful of all P's professional goals because it is reassuring for P and reminds P that P has something to give to others, which adds meaning to P's life. P likes that P can immediately see the value a client places on being heard by P. P finds a lot of meaning in hearing someone who does not get heard by others.

VB I21-P21: Now P realizes feeling emotions strongly leads P to be more intuitive and able to feel what other people were feeling, which works to P's advantage as a therapist. P is good at being a therapist and cannot see herself being better at anything than therapy.

VB I22-P22: P needs to believe P is actually useful and helping people. P needs to feel P is having an impact on people's lives, helping them to break out of maladaptive cycles. Helping people individually and breaking maladaptive cycles gives P meaning.

VB I33-P33: Therapy gives P a feeling of self-efficacy; P knows what P is doing.

VB I59-P60: P values being a positive role model. P derives meaning from giving others hope and impacting others positively. It is meaningful to give others hope to provide an internal stimulus for change. People have the capacity to heal themselves but often need someone to guide them through the process, and P derives meaning from being that person.

MC I9-P12: P thought about meaning in life in terms of career goals.

MC I17-P19: P's career is fulfilling, which gives a lot of meaning.

MC I23-P27: P wants to be a writer, be involved in a multicultural minority student organization as a volunteer, provide free counseling, fundraise and organize educational activities, and write a children's book because children have so much potential and P wants to influence them.

MC I28-P29: P wants to be a therapist to "help people fulfill their potentials, to encourage them to live whatever lives they want, and to have women to make their own choices."

MC I37-P39: P believes that providing therapy helps P focus on the present, and that helps P feel like P is fully living by helping others. P feels useful and self-efficacious when P helps someone grow or overcome their obstacles through therapy. P thinks therapy is surreal because P sees other perspectives and experiences. P feels therapy provides P with connection to others and creates a safe and supportive atmosphere.

MC I41-P41: P thinks therapist training helped P become a better person by being able to communicate emotions. Therapist training helped personal growth, which is meaningful to P.

Note. Initials refer to codes used to identify interviewees (based on interviewers' initials). Numbers refer to line numbers in the interview transcript.

EXHIBIT 6.3. Example of Cross-Analysis for Two Cases Domain 1: "Being a Therapist as a Source of Meaning in Life"

1. Being a therapist

    1.a. Self-oriented meanings from being a therapist

        1a.i. Feels fulfilled and efficacious

            VB I33-P33: Therapy gives P a feeling of self-efficacy; P knows what P is doing. I13-P13: P finds being a therapist the most meaningful of all P's professional goals because it is reassuring for P and reminds P that P has something to give to others, which adds meaning to P's life. P11: P believes that completely immersing self with a client gives meaning in life.

            MC I37-P39: P believes that providing therapy helps her focus on the present and that helps P feel like P is fully living by helping others. P feels useful and self-efficacious when P helps someone grow or overcome their obstacles through therapy.

        1.a.ii. Provides personal growth and insight

            VB I21-P21: Now P realizes feeling emotions strongly leads P to be more intuitive and able to feel what other people were feeling, which works to P's advantage as a therapist.

            MC I37-P39: P thinks therapy is surreal because P sees other perspectives and experiences. I41-P41: P thinks therapist training helped P become a better person by being able to communicate emotions. Therapist training helped personal growth, which is meaningful to P.

        1.a.iii. Allows for connection and intimacy [As noted earlier, categories and themes must have at least two cases. Across these two case examples, however, only one had data that fit into this category or theme. When later cases were added in, additional cores were placed here, thus justifying this category or theme.]

            MC I37-P39: P feels therapy provides P with connection to others and creates a safe and supportive atmosphere.

        1.a.iv. Fulfills a talent

            VB I21-P21: P is good at being a therapist and cannot see herself being better at anything than therapy.

            MC I17-P19: P's career is fulfilling which gives P a lot of meaning.

    1.b. Other-oriented meanings from being a therapist

        1.b.i. Helps others

            VB I13-P13: P likes that P can immediately see the value a client places on being heard by P. P finds a lot of meaning in hearing someone who does not get heard by others. I22-P22: P needs to believe P is actually useful and helping people. P needs to feel P is having an impact on people's lives, helping them to break out of maladaptive cycles. Helping people individually and breaking maladaptive cycles gives meaning. I59-P60: P values being a positive role model. P derives meaning from giving others hope and impacting others

(continues)

EXHIBIT 6.3. Example of Cross-Analysis for Two Cases Domain 1: "Being a Therapist as a Source of Meaning in Life" (*Continued*)

positively. It is meaningful to give others hope to provide an internal stimulus for change. People have the capacity to heal themselves but often need someone to guide them through the process, and P derives meaning from being that person.

MC I28–P29: P wants to be a therapist to "help people fulfill their potentials, to encourage them to live whatever lives they want, and to have women make their own choices."

1.b.ii. Make the world a better place [See earlier note regarding having only one case here.]

MC I23–P27: P wants to be involved in a multicultural minority student organization as a volunteer, provide free counseling, fundraise and organize educational activities, and write a children's book because children have so much potential and P wants to influence them.

Note. Initials refer to codes used to identify interviewees (based on interviewers' initials). Numbers refer to line numbers in the interview transcript.

THE AUDIT

The primary team submits its work to the auditor(s). Typically, we ask the auditors to review each domain as we complete it and then, in addition, review all domains together at the end to see how they all fit together. Auditors examine whether the titles of categories and subcategories make sense and whether the core ideas placed under the categories and subcategories fit the titles. When examining the whole cross-analysis (i.e., at the end of the data analysis process, after each domain's cross-analysis has been individually audited), the auditors are seeking concise elegance of the structure of the cross-analysis. They want to see whether there are too many general categories that could be subdivided or too many variant categories that could be collapsed into larger categories. Across the analysis, the auditors also examine whether data core ideas in the "Other" category could be placed in existing categories and whether new categories are needed.

The primary team considers the auditor's suggestions and modifies the cross-analysis accordingly. The primary team and the auditors may have to correspond numerous times until the most elegant depiction of the findings in the cross-analysis emerges. We find it helpful to sit with the entire cross-analysis and reflect on it as we continue to see new patterns in the data.

Representativeness of Themes

Frequency information is noted to reflect the number of participants whose core ideas fit within each category or subcategory. Although there may be more than one core idea for one participant, we count each participant only once per category or subcategory.

When a category consists of data from all or all but one of the participants, that category is labeled "general"; categories that consist of data from more than half of the participants up to the cutoff for general are labeled "typical"; categories that consist of data from at least two participants up to half of the participants are considered "variant." For example, with 13 participants, evidence for 12 or 13 cases is considered general, seven to 11 typical, and two to six variant. When samples are larger than 15, we sometimes include a category of "rare" for two to three participants (in which case, variant would contain at least four and up to half of the participants). The general, typical, and variant (and rare, if used) labels work better than percentages or raw frequencies because they allow for comparisons across studies and reduce the tendency to overinterpret a specific percentage or number as meaningful. When we write up the data, however, we provide both the frequency label (general, typical, variant), as well as the frequency so that readers have full information about the extent to which the category applied to the sample.

We do not usually report data that emerges for only one case (these usually go into an "Other" category) unless that case stands out in some particular way that we want to highlight. For example, in the study about client perspectives about giving gifts to therapists (Knox et al., 2003), one client stood out as having given many expensive gifts to her therapist. In the manuscript, we highlighted this case because it illustrated an important finding about problematic gift giving.

In the final table, the categories and subcategories within domains are listed in descending order of frequency, with designations next to each regarding whether it was general (G), typical (T), variant (V), or rare (R) and listing the frequency. The "Other" category is not listed in the final table. See Exhibit 6.4 for an example of a section of a cross-analysis table related to the domain of being a therapist as a source of meaning.

Describing and Comparing Subsamples

Delineating subsamples is useful when researchers recognize that participants differ in some meaningful and noticeable manner, and this differentiation helps reduce the variability in the data. For example, in the sexual attraction study (Ladany et al., 1997), about half the participants disclosed to their supervisor that they felt sexually attracted to a client, whereas the other half did not disclose this information. Comparing the subsamples

EXHIBIT 6.4. Final Table for Domain 1: "Being a Therapist as a Source of Meaning in Life" (Including All Participants)

Being a therapist	
Self-oriented meanings	
Feels fulfilled or efficacious	General (9)
Leads to personal growth or insight	General (9)
Allows for connection and intimacy	Typical (7)
Fulfills a talent	Variant (4)
Other-oriented meanings	
Help others	General (10)
Make a better world	Typical (8)

provided meaningful information that helped us understand the phenomenon of sexual attraction more completely.

We stress, however, that we first do the cross-analysis on all the data combined and only divide the sample into subsamples after the initial cross-analysis is completed. In this way, the same categories are used for the whole sample, and comparisons can be made more easily across subsamples. When characterizing the subsamples, the same criteria for general, typical, and variant are used (see earlier), but the specific number to determine the general, typical, and variant designations differs according to the total number of cases in each subsample.

We emphasize that subsample analyses can only be done if the subsamples are relatively large (e.g., at least seven participants). Subsamples with few participants lead to findings that are often unstable (i.e., would vary considerably across samples).

We have developed a criterion that subsamples have to differ by at least 30% of cases (this difference is fairly large) to be considered meaningfully different (Ladany et al., 2012). For example, we would consider subsamples to be different if a category emerged for 80% of the participants in one subsample but for only 50% in another subsample. It is important that researchers set this 30% criterion a priori so that they are not basing this decision on whether they "like" the results of the subsample comparison.

Troubleshooting During the Cross-Analysis

During the cross-analysis process, researchers keep a keen eye on the emerging category structure. In particular, researchers seek to avoid category structures that produce either all or no general categories or a preponderance of variant categories. In either of these circumstances, the emerging cross-analysis may not represent the data adequately. For instance, cross-analyses that contain primarily general categories may profit from including more subcategories to describe the data more fully. In contrast, cross-analyses with mostly variant categories may indicate that the sample was too heterogeneous or that the team was too microscopic in its development of categories; it may be necessary to collect more data and/or to reexamine the level of specificity in the categories themselves.

Poor category structures can also emerge from poor interviews (e.g., if the interviewers did not follow the protocol, failed to probe and ask participants to elaborate or clarify statements, or prompted the participant too much) or from a problematic protocol (e.g., a large number of questions that might have been too broad or narrow in scope). This outcome can be discouraging given the time invested in the data collection and analysis, but it is nevertheless a good learning experience for better designing future studies. We admit that some of our studies have never been published because of critical design or interview flaws.

Checking for Stability

In our first article on CQR (Hill et al., 1997), we recommended holding out two cases when doing the initial cross-analysis. These cases were later added after the initial cross-analysis to determine whether their addition made a difference. If no differences emerged when the new cases were added, we could feel comfortable that stability (called "saturation" by other qualitative researchers) had been achieved and further similar cases would not radically change the findings.

In our review of the studies using CQR (Hill et al., 2005), we found that most investigators were not including the stability check. Furthermore, we noted that the criteria to be used for stability checks were not clear: How many differences are needed to determine that data are not stable? What exactly is a difference? It was difficult to know what criteria to use to determine whether "new" information truly emerged, and we noticed a tendency on the part of researchers to minimize the possibility that new findings had emerged after the long data analysis process. Because all interviews are typically conducted at about the same time before data analysis in CQR (rather than intertwined with the analysis process, as is done in grounded theory), it would introduce many potential confounds into a study if researchers were to conduct additional interviews at a later time after data analysis, given that the research team would have new biases based on their experiences with the data analysis, and knowledge of the initial results could influence the interview process. Hence, we no longer recommend holding out cases for a stability check (see also Hill et al., 2005).

Of course, we acknowledge that consistency of results (stability) is valuable. We thus try to assure consistency and trustworthiness of results by (a) carefully constructing the interview protocol to ask clear questions, (b) training interviewers to be consistent across interviews, (c) conducting pilot interviews to ensure that we are getting valuable data, (d) carefully defining and recruiting a relatively large sample of participants (approximately 13 to 15), and (e) carefully conducting the data analysis with several team members and auditors to get multiple perspectives. In our experience, we have found that new categories and subcategories rarely emerge after 10 or 11 cases have been included in the cross-analyses, suggesting stability or saturation, which is what we hope to see. In addition, if we find general and typical categories, we feel more certain that we have obtained representative data.

CONCLUSIONS

Many, then, are the challenges of conducting the cross-analysis because it demands a different level of analysis than the within-case processes of developing domains and core ideas. For us, though, this is the most fun part of the data analysis because we finally begin to see the hopefully exciting findings that the study has yielded.

7 WRITING THE MANUSCRIPT

Although there are no strict "rules" for writing a consensual qualitative research (CQR) manuscript, our goal here is to help readers think about the decisions they will make in preparing their manuscripts. We follow the general guidelines outlined in the *Publication Manual of the American Psychological Association* (American Psychological Association, 2020) and in the guidelines for reporting qualitative research (Levitt et al., 2018). We note, however, that journal culture and customs vary, so it is important to become familiar with the particular journal to which you will be submitting the manuscript.

INTRODUCTION

The Introduction is usually relatively brief, between five to 10 pages. The Introduction is like a legal argument, leading the reader to see the need for this particular study.

The first task in the Introduction is to define the topic and provide a justification for the importance of its examination. By the end of the first page, the reader should be given a clear idea of the overall rationale and purpose of the study. The second task is to briefly review the relevant literature,

https://doi.org/10.1037/0000215-007
Essentials of Consensual Qualitative Research, by C. E. Hill and S. Knox

noting the key findings and limitations of previous research. In the final section, researchers state the purposes and research questions, as well as justify the unique aspects of their study (e.g., choice of sample). We also recommend providing a clear rationale for the choice of a qualitative approach in general and CQR specifically, the latter of which can highlight the strengths of CQR vis-à-vis other qualitative methods (e.g., consensus, multiple perspectives, external auditors, rigor).

As noted earlier in the book, we encourage authors to write a draft of the Introduction before collecting data to help them think through the rationale, literature, and procedures. Then, we suggest you set this aside during the data collection and analysis phases. When writing up the rest of the manuscript, we suggest you come back and modify this section according to all the changes you made during the project.

METHOD

Authors start the Method section by describing the data set, noting any unusual features (e.g., particular requirements that potential participants must meet). They then describe the participants themselves (interviewees, interviewers, primary research team, auditors) in terms of age, race, ethnicity, gender, and other characteristics relevant to the study. In addition, for the interviewers, research team, and auditors, authors describe previous experiences, biases, and expectations related to the topic so that readers can understand how these might influence the results.

Next, authors provide detail about measures. They include a description of the interview protocol and how it was developed. They also describe any standardized measures that may have been included to situate the sample or triangulate results.

Finally, the authors describe the procedures, including how participants were recruited and the key steps of CQR (e.g., domains, core ideas, cross-analysis). If authors deviate from the CQR method, they should describe and justify these changes. Enough detail about CQR should be included in the Method section so that readers know what was done, and other researchers could replicate the method and compare results with other studies.

RESULTS

The Results section offers the opportunity for authors to continue to work with and explore the data by presenting them in a clear manner. New ways of viewing the data often occur to researchers as they start writing the results (e.g., they may discover a more clear and compelling way to "tell the story" of their findings). Researchers may also realize that some of their understandings of the data warrant further examination, and thus they can return to the data and rethink various analytic decisions. Immersing oneself in the data at this point is necessary for understanding the data, so we recommend against dividing this task among several people.

An initial decision in preparing a CQR manuscript is deciding which findings to present. CQR researchers often collect and analyze more data than they can include in a single manuscript, given the space limitations in journals. Thus, they must decide which findings best answer their research questions and which are more peripheral and could be omitted from the manuscript. For example, we often do not include data related to warm-up questions (e.g., "Please tell me about your experience of this therapy" in a study examining clients' experiences of therapy termination; Knox, Adrians, et al., 2011) or wrap-up questions (e.g., "Why did you participate in this study?" "What was your experience of participating in this study?") in the manuscript unless they were particularly salient for some reason. Of course, authors should inform readers about what findings they have chosen not to report and their reasons for doing this.

In this section, authors present each domain and the categories (themes) found for that domain (e.g., under the domain of experiences of deliberate practice training, we had categories of helpful and unhelpful experiences, each of which was further subdivided; Hill, Kivlighan, et al., 2019). They describe each category (and subcategory) and then provide one or two excerpts (quotes) from the actual interviews so that readers can judge the evidence for these categories. We also suggest that authors provide at least one or two illustrative whole-case examples (anonymized so that identity cannot be determined) so that readers obtain a feeling for all the data in context. Finally, we recommend including a table with all domains and categories and subcategories so that readers can follow the structure of the findings.

DISCUSSION

In the Discussion section, authors interpret the findings in relation to the literature and note their importance and implications. A challenge that regularly besets CQR researchers is how to craft a Discussion section that weaves the findings into a compelling story rather than simply repeating the results. One strategy we have used is to identify three to five essential "take-home" messages and expand on these results. Paring down the data into juicy nuggets forces researchers to distill their findings to the most fundamental essence that links to the research questions guiding the study and also to the extant literature. For instance, in a manuscript on supervisees' experience of supervisor self-disclosure (Knox, Edwards, et al., 2011), the components that appeared to contribute most to the positive or problematic effects of such disclosures were the supervisory relationship, supervisors' responsiveness to supervisees' needs or concerns, and appropriate and clear intentions for the disclosure. Those components then served as the scaffolding for the entire Discussion section. Another strategy is to weave together the findings into a new theoretical structure, much as would be found in a grounded theory approach (see Schlosser et al., 2003, for a good example).

After interpreting their findings in the Discussion section, CQR authors note the limitations of their research to enable readers to consider the results within that context (remembering that every study has limitations). Authors acknowledge anything unusual about the sample, especially if that sample was heterogeneous or anomalous in some way (e.g., age, sex, race, ethnicity, experience related to the topic of study), and caution their audience about generalizing the findings to the larger population. Authors also address particular features of the research team and/or the participant sample (e.g., minimal racial or ethnic diversity) and posit the possible effects of such differences. In addition, authors speak here about the potential impact of their identities, experiences, and biases or expectations on their understanding and analysis of the data. For example, different research teams, with different characteristics, might arrive at slightly different results. In a study of advisors' positive and problematic dissertation experiences (Knox, Burkard, et al., 2011), for instance, we noted that the faculty on the primary team had minimal experience as dissertation advisors at the time of the research and that the team members had mixed experiences in working with their advisors on their dissertations. We acknowledged that these experiences could have biased our interpretation of the data but also noted that the use of experienced external auditors reduced the likelihood of misperceptions.

In the final section of the Discussion, the authors describe the implications of their work, being careful not to go too far beyond their data. In an investigation of client gifts to therapists (Knox et al., 2009), for example, the authors noted that because giving a small gift and processing this experience can have potent effects on the therapy process, such gift giving must be managed with sensitivity. The authors also reminded readers of the experiences of the one participant whose therapist appeared to solicit gifts, further strengthening the need for care in such interactions. Authors conclude by offering implications for further research, training, and/or practice, thereby helping others think of ways to expand the research.

GENERAL CONSIDERATIONS

Generally, the first author writes the manuscript to provide a consistent "voice" across the sections, with other team members providing feedback on the drafts before submission for publication. Occasionally, however, different team members write different sections (e.g., Introduction, Method) of the paper, although it is then important to make sure that the whole paper has a consistent voice.

We suggest having people external to the research team provide a critical review of the manuscript to provide a fresh perspective. These external reviewers can be selected for their content area expertise and familiarity with CQR and should be cited in the Author Notes section. Similarly, it can be helpful to present the research at professional conferences before submitting it for publication. Preparing for an oral presentation enables authors to focus on the essential findings and present them in a way that is compelling for the audience. An additional benefit of such presentations is receiving feedback, which might facilitate the generation of new ideas and perspectives. Given that acceptance for publication is highly competitive, getting feedback ahead of time can enhance the prospect of manuscripts being accepted for publication. Furthermore, when your manuscript is rejected at one journal (as is common), do not despair; use the feedback to rewrite the manuscript and submit it to another journal.

CONCLUSIONS

Writing the manuscript is both one of the most fun parts as well as one of the most challenging parts of CQR projects. It is enjoyable to see the findings all come together and communicate them to a broader audience, but it is challenging to condense the wealth of data and impressions into a coherent story. We rewrite many times before submitting the paper and solicit plentiful feedback to make sure we are communicating the results in the best possible way.

8 VARIATIONS ON CONSENSUAL QUALITATIVE RESEARCH

In this chapter, we first describe modifications of consensual qualitative research (CQR) for comparatively simple data and single-case data. Then, we describe a method we have developed for qualitative meta-analysis to compare results across studies. Finally, we offer some ideas about other possible modifications.

CQR-M

Sometimes, researchers ask participants to respond to open-ended questions in writing, most often at the end of surveys. One purpose of such data gathering is to encourage participants to expand on their answers to the questionnaires so that the researchers can acquire individualized information not captured by standardized measures. If multiple methods are used within a study (e.g., questionnaire data followed by open-ended questions analyzed via CQR-modified [CQR-M]), results can be compared across methods (also called triangulation; Denzin, 1978). Another purpose is to collect some qualitative data from a large number of participants but admittedly without the depth achieved in an interview. Thus, in contrast to the rich, intensive interview data from a few participants that we acquire with regular CQR,

https://doi.org/10.1037/0000215-008
Essentials of Consensual Qualitative Research, by C. E. Hill and S. Knox

these data are more brief and superficial responses. Hence, we can use a modified form of CQR (Spangler et al., 2012) to analyze the data.

Definition and Background

Before the development of CQR-M (and as noted in Chapter 1), the alternative means of working with simple data was to have one team of judges create categories from the data and then have another team of judges independently code the data into those categories and only accept the codings if the judges attained high interrater reliability (e.g., Hill, 1990; Mahrer, 1988). We favor CQR-M over methods that emphasize interrater agreement for several reasons. First, CQR-M judges discuss their expectations, biases, and disagreements with each other before data analysis and can thus help each other keep accountable to the data. In addition, because human communication is often nuanced and ambiguous, being able to think and talk about shades of meaning and consensually code the data helps researchers arrive at a more faithful representation of participants' responses than can typically be achieved by coders working independently (as they would if required to obtain high interrater agreement). Last, when high interrater reliability is required, judges often consciously or unconsciously constrain their clinical intuition and try to guess what other judges will say so that they can attain a high level of agreement.

In contrast, with CQR-M, judges are not required to force data into particular categories just to attain high agreement levels (Hill et al., 1997). Instead, they are encouraged to use their experience and wisdom to provide thoughtful reasons for their coding and also to listen to others and negotiate the best understanding of the data. Having multiple perspectives thus minimizes individual biases and thereby may yield a better understanding of the data.

For example, in a study on immediacy training (Spangler et al., 2014), the overall purpose of the study was to investigate how specific instructional components contributed to students' self-efficacy for using immediacy. After engaging in each component of training (e.g., reading, lecture, practice), participants rated their self-efficacy for using immediacy using a four-item measure. We triangulated these quantitative results with CQR-M–analyzed results of participants' responses at the end of training to several open-ended questions ("What was most helpful about the training?" "What was least helpful?"). Interestingly, qualitative and quantitative analyses revealed somewhat different results, perhaps because the self-efficacy measure was completed immediately after each component of training, whereas the open-ended questions were administered at the end of the entire training. Quantitative results showed that the greatest increase in self-efficacy was after the lecture component, whereas CQR-M analyses indicated that 72% of the sample believed that practice was the most effective part of the training. Clearly, then, the qualitative component in this study raised interesting questions about the comparative effectiveness of the various instructional components and the timing of the assessments of the learning.

Development of Open-Ended Questions

A major departure of CQR-M is that the researcher's relationship to the participant is less a factor than it is with CQR, given that written open-ended questions are typically used rather than interviews. Thus, it is crucial that the open-ended questions are crafted well to yield good data.

In developing the questions for CQR-M, researchers must have a clear idea of what information they want to gather. Depending on the purpose, steering a course between specificity and openness will inform the construction of the questions. It is important to ask just one question at a time and to think of this question as a domain (major topic). For example, if researchers are interested in attitudes toward seeking mental health treatment, they might ask a question about what barriers the person has to seeking mental health treatment and another question about how others might perceive them if they sought mental health treatment.

If control over the scope and length of responses is desired, a set amount of space can be provided for participants to write their answers. For example, in the aforementioned Spangler et al. (2014) study, participants were given half a page in which to type their responses to each question, thus indicating to them the expected length of their responses and providing a degree of consistency in the scope of responses. Alternatively, participants could be told to write a specific amount (e.g., at least three sentences) in response to the question. In our experience, if nothing specific about length is stated, participants often skip the open-ended questions to save time.

As with CQR, CQR-M researchers pilot their questions to ensure that potential participants understand what is being asked and can provide good information. After developing their questions, researchers articulate their biases and expectations (see Chapter 2).

The Coding Process

Categories and subcategories for each of the questions (domains) are directly derived from the raw data. Note that core ideas are not needed here because the responses to the open-ended questions are usually short and not complicated and thus do not need to be interpreted. Rather, judges can simply place the raw data directly into the categories and subcategories.

Typically, we have at least two people read through a subset of responses to each question (domain) and identify categories (and subcategories, if appropriate) that emerge. They stop when no new categories or subcategories seem to be emerging. They then create an initial list of categories and subcategories for each domain, putting similar categories close together.

A new team of at least three judges then discusses each of the domains, categories, and subcategories to reach a common understanding of their meaning, modifying the categories as necessary to provide more clarity. They then apply the modified categories to a different subset of the data to see how well the categories fit these new data, modifying as necessary. They use the consensus process as described for CQR.

Once the domains and categories are well established, the team of judges codes the rest of the data, including recoding the subsets of data used to develop the initial category system. Once the data are coded, auditors review the codes and raw data.

The next step in CQR-M analyses is to determine the response frequency, which we do by somewhat arbitrarily presenting the proportion of participants represented in each category (the number of participants represented in each category divided by the total number of participants), as well as determining whether frequencies are general (90%–100%), typical (51%–89%), variant (21%–50%), or rare (1%–10%). We can then assess differences between categories using the a priori criterion of 30% described in Chapter 3. For example, in the immediacy training study (Spangler et al., 2014), 72% of the sample indicated that practice was a helpful component of the immediacy training, whereas only 14% indicated that lecture was helpful. Given that the difference was more than 30%, we concluded that participants found practice more helpful than lecture.

As a final step, we examine our category structure to determine whether it is as elegant as possible. We look for categories that have only a few participants, seem minor, or overlap with other categories. We might combine small categories into larger, more abstract categories; we may put small, less relevant, infrequently occurring categories into an "Other" category; we might subdivide large complex categories.

The final steps of a CQR-M project would be similar to that of a regular CQR study. These include writing the manuscript, being careful to include the limitations of the relatively superficial nature of the qualitative data.

CQR FOR CASE STUDY RESEARCH

Although an interview approach is excellent for directly asking participants about their experiences, attitudes, or beliefs, it is not adequate for analyzing phenomena that are best observed as they occur (e.g., events in psychotherapy sessions) and for which we have not directly asked participants about their experiences. Because psychotherapy researchers are interested in qualitatively analyzing data obtained through the observation of events within cases of psychotherapy, Jackson et al. (2012) developed CQR for case study research (CQR-C). Our initial efforts in using CQR-C involved having a team of researchers study a case (or cases) and rate via consensus the process specific events using existing or created measures. We then summarized the data (e.g., ratings of the depth of client response to therapist immediacy, Hill et al., 2014; ratings of client involvement before and after silence, Hill, Kline, et al., 2019) using statistical analyses. Although this approach goes a step beyond traditional quantitatively oriented process research in that it involves consensus, it remains essentially a quantitative approach. We have been evolving CQR-C through a series of studies and are just arriving at a fairly solid approach, which we present here, for working with case data from an observational, qualitative perspective, one that is similar to interpretive phenomenological analyses (Smith & Nizza, in press).

As with CQR, CQR-C offers researchers both rigor and depth in the examination and description of complex phenomena and invites in-depth discussion among research team members to reach consensus judgments. Each team member's experience of the case is thus invoked and incorporated to yield a rich understanding of a phenomenon. We define a *case study* as research focusing on the unfolding of phenomena of interest over a single case or across a small number of cases (a multiple case study).

Getting Started

Identifying a clear topic is critical to obtaining rich, meaningful results in CQR-C, just as it is in CQR. The topic also guides the selection of an appropriate case and identification of the events of interest within the case (e.g., if you wish to study therapist use of silence, you have to pick a case where therapist silence occurs). Once a topic has been selected, researchers develop research questions to guide the study (although these questions typically change as researchers immerse themselves in the case and refine their focus). Examples of the research questions for a current CQR-C study on therapist challenges are "What types of challenges are used?" and "How do clients respond to therapist challenges?"

The optimal research team comprises members who have had experience, either through training or professional work, with the phenomenon and CQR. We like using large teams (e.g., four to eight members) because several perspectives are valuable when observing complicated data and because we have not used auditors. It is helpful to choose team members who differ in level of expertise, given that novice members can add a fresh perspective, and more seasoned members can offer wisdom from their experience. We recommend against having the therapist serve on the research team because it is often hard for others to openly discuss the process when the therapist involved in the case is present. Once a team has been selected, the researchers discuss their biases and expectations about the topic (see Chapter 3).

Researchers have two main options for obtaining case material. If they are interested in studying psychotherapy phenomena, for example, they can recruit a client and therapist to complete a course of therapy for the purposes of the study (e.g., in the study of therapist immediacy in brief psychotherapy, Kasper et al., 2008, recruited both an interpersonally oriented psychotherapist and a client who responded positively to probes for immediacy during a recruitment interview). A second option is to select a case from an archival data set (e.g., Berman et al., 2012, investigated how relational work unfolded in an existing set of three cases of acceptance and commitment therapy with clients who had anorexia nervosa). An important caveat is that it is useful to have videotapes rather than just audiotapes of sessions so that judges have access to both the verbal and nonverbal behavior, given that how things are said modifies the communication itself (e.g., tone of voice and nonverbal gestures can make a therapist intervention a challenge even when the words on paper sound supportive).

Preparing for Data Collection

Researchers first familiarize themselves with the case to obtain a context for later judgments about the topic. Watching the videos of the entire case is sometimes helpful, although it could be problematic if awareness of later events and the outcome of the case biases judgments. In such instances, it may be preferable for team members to familiarize themselves with the case by watching the intake and early sessions. We write a conceptualization of the case based on these early sessions so that we have the context of the case before proceeding with the analyses of the particular topic.

We usually investigate the evolving nature of a specific type of event across therapy (e.g., how silence changes across therapy). An *event* is a segment in a session of therapy where the phenomenon of interest occurs. An event is defined by its beginning (e.g., when the phenomenon initially appears or starts) and its end (e.g., when the phenomenon disappears or ends). For example, in Hill et al.'s (2008) study of immediacy in psychotherapy, an immediacy event began when either the therapist or client initiated a discussion of the therapeutic relationship, and the other person accepted the bid to engage in the discussion; the event ended when the discussion shifted to another topic. If the discussion about the topic was resumed later in the session, it was coded as either the same event or a separate event depending on the similarity of the content (i.e., if participants returned to the topic after an interlude such as "As I was saying earlier," we counted that as a continuation of the same event, whereas if participants said something like "That incident reminds me of another incident," we would code that as a separate event). Each event can range from a few seconds to several sessions.

Data Analysis

The procedures described in this section are those we have evolved in our current study on challenges in therapy. We expect that our procedures will continue to evolve as we test them out in further studies, but we hope that this section provides enough information for other researchers to get started.

Once the team has the background and context of the case, they watch sessions of a case sequentially (so that they have a sense of the context and unfolding of the case). They stop the tape when team members identify the occurrence of an event. They record the beginning and end of the event, rewatch the event, and prepare a narrative description of the event (e.g., "The therapist asked the client how he felt about her arriving late for the session. The client felt upset because he thought that the therapist didn't respect him or care about him. He noted that the therapist had been late two other times. The therapist apologized for being late and stated that she did respect the client and was invested in their work"). Consensus is important in developing the narrative description because it ensures that the perspectives of all team members are reflected. To encourage each team member to have an equal voice, team members rotate providing initial descriptions of events.

Next, the team replays and rewatches the relevant segment of the video and discusses their interpretation of this segment. This discussion is much like the interview for CQR and can include a few standard questions, as well as allowing the team to be free floating about whatever else they might want to address according to the individual case. Thus, for the antecedents to the event, they might ask: (a) "What was going on before the event?" and (b) "What were the interpersonal dynamics between the therapist and client?" Similar questions and procedures would be used to interrogate the event, the consequences, and anything else of interest.

The choice of the number of events to include depends on the topic. We suggest, however, that researchers include a relatively large number of events if there is variation across events. Inclusion of more events, and then subdividing the events in some way, can help the researchers make sense of the factors that influence the events. For instance, the researchers might examine 15 events from early in therapy, 15 events from the middle of therapy, and 15 events from the end of therapy to see whether there are differences across time.

At the end of this process, the team will have a lot of data about each event. They can return to the events and make sure they have included a consistent amount of information about each event. They could also add questions to assess delayed effects across time. They likely also have to edit their answers to these questions to ensure that everything is clear, returning to the video and transcripts as needed to check for clarity. In essence, they now have what we referred to in CQR as a consensus version, such that there are core ideas (written responses) within the questions (which now become domains).

Now the team conducts a cross-analysis, looking for themes within domains (see Chapter 6). For example, in a case study of a client expressing anger toward a therapist, the typical antecedent might be the client demanding advice and the therapist not providing it, whereas a variant antecedent might be the therapist making an error (e.g., being late, committing a micro-aggression). In all cases, the client might have responded with anger (because that was the focus of the study, all events were chosen to reflect this emotion). The event itself might also, however, involve the therapist and client interactions about the anger. Perhaps the typical response would be for the therapist to respond with hostility to the client's anger, whereas a variant response would be for the therapist to apologize and help the client explore and process the event. Consequences might typically involve a failure to resolve the rupture and variantly involve a resolution of the event. The typical pattern across events might be the client demanding advice, the therapist not giving advice, the client getting angry, the therapist responding with hostility to the request, and a resulting lack of resolution. A variant pattern might be the therapist making an error, the client getting covertly angry, the therapist apologizing and helping the client process the experience, and a resulting repair of the rupture.

We also suggest writing a narrative about the findings across events to include overall impressions of the case. For example, in the study on interpretations and probes for insight (Hill et al., 2020), our team wrote a narrative about these therapist skills within the context of the treatment process for the client with each of three therapists. First, team members independently wrote narratives, which they read aloud at a team meeting, with others asking for more details and explanation but no criticism. One person then compiled the narratives, and team members provided feedback until the team arrived at a consensus version summarizing the discussions about the phenomenon as it manifested in the case.

As a final step, we ask case-study participants to read the manuscript (in which names and factual information have been anonymized to protect confidentiality). This step is important ethically so that participants can give their final approval about what is being published from their data. Interestingly, writing the manuscript knowing that participants will read it forces authors to be compassionate and take the participants' perspectives. We send the manuscript to participants and then meet either in person or by phone for an individual 1-hour interview, during which we ask whether they feel comfortable with the content from their case included in the paper and whether they have any questions, and we ask any remaining questions we have of them. We have found that these interviews add considerably to our understanding of the cases and give us a chance to thank the participants.

QUALITATIVE META-ANALYSES OF CQR STUDIES

Any single CQR study can be informative and important, but we cannot neglect questions about the representativeness of findings beyond the specific sample. For science to advance, we need to know the consistency of findings across samples. Thus, like others who developed methods for qualitative meta-analysis or meta-synthesis (e.g., Timulak, 2009), Hill et al. (2012) developed a method for conducting qualitative meta-analyses (QMA).

We illustrate QMA through our review of therapist self-disclosure and immediacy (Hill et al., 2018). Just as quantitative meta-analysts (see Berkeljon & Baldwin, 2009) first examine overall effects and then explore particular features of subsamples, our aims with QMA are to summarize overall findings and then explore differences across subsamples.

Data Collection

We recommend having three to four people on a QMA research team to allow for a variety of opinions. In terms of qualifications for the team, experience with CQR is most relevant, along with expertise in the topic being investigated.

To facilitate fair comparisons across studies, researchers select studies that address the same topic. For example, all selected studies might address why participants chose to participate in the research, helpful aspects of psychotherapy, or experiences of crying in psychotherapy. Researchers next determine inclusion and exclusion criteria to determine what studies to include in the QMA. For instance, they might decide to include only studies that faithfully followed CQR and exclude studies that did not include quotations to illustrate categories and did not report numbers or percentages in addition to frequency labels (e.g., general, typical) because it is difficult to summarize studies without frequency numbers. Researchers then exhaustively search the literature (both through database searches and asking colleagues about unpublished studies) to make sure that they include all eligible published and unpublished studies.

The decision about the number of studies needed for a QMA depends on the reason for conducting the QMA. If the intent is to feel confident about the findings in a particular area, many studies are needed (e.g., Paterson et al., 2001, recommended at least a dozen studies) to obtain stable results. In addition, if the purpose of the QMA is to investigate the effects of specific features of the studies (e.g., type of sample), ideally, there would be at least eight studies of each type so that potential differences among examined features could emerge with some stability. If the purpose, however, is to perform a preliminary comparison of findings across studies in an area where few studies exist, as few as three studies could be included in the QMA.

Aggregating Results Across Studies

The first step is to list all the results found in each study and indicate the percentage of participants for whom the results applied. If the original researchers did not provide percentages in addition to labels such as general, typical, and variant, QMA researchers can estimate by using the middle number of the label (e.g., if a typical category consisted of five to seven participants, researchers would use six as the estimate).

Next, researchers reach consensus regarding whether categories from one study are similar to or distinct from categories in other studies, essentially doing a cross-analysis of the cross-analyses. For example, in the Hill et al. (2018) QMA, we consensually agreed that all categories related to aspects of the therapeutic relationship (e.g., supported, gained trust, more real relationship) would be clustered together into a larger, more inclusive category about the therapeutic relationship, but we distinguished this category from other categories such as "gained insight." Reading the descriptions of the categories and the quotations is essential here to determine the degree of similarity in the content of categories across studies.

At the end of this step, researchers will have generated a list of common categories across studies. They can then determine the average number of participants across studies for each category (e.g., the total number of participants who endorsed a particular category divided by the total number of participants across all studies, recalling that each participant counts only once per category). They can then label results as general, typical, or variant across studies (in a general category, at least 90% of participants across all cases are represented in that category; in a typical category, between 51% and 89% of participants across all cases are represented; in a variant category, between 20% and 50% of participants across all cases are represented). Researchers now have the evidence about the overall results across studies.

Comparing Subsamples

Rarely are all studies clear replications of each other. Rather, there are many unique features of studies in terms of samples and data collection methods, all of which can influence the data. Hence, researchers can check for whether there are subsample differences if there are enough studies. For example, in the Hill et al. (2018) QMA, we looked for whether results differed according to whether the therapist interventions were self-disclosures or immediacy (given that some studies focused on self-disclosure, others on immediacy, and still others included both). In describing such differences, and as earlier noted, we decided a priori that we would consider a difference between subsamples to be meaningful if it differed by at least 30% of the participants (because a difference that large seemed unlikely to have occurred by chance). This analysis showed that self-disclosures were associated more often than immediacy with better client mental health functioning (45% vs. 9%), enhanced therapeutic relationship (64% vs. 23%), and overall helpfulness (37% vs. 5%) but less often with clients opening up (27% vs. 60%) and client immediacy (0% vs. 55%).

Final Product

As with CQR-M and CQR-C, the product of a QMA is a written publication summarizing the results. This manuscript would follow the style presented in Chapter 7 of this book and would essentially look like a cross-analysis of all the cross-analyses.

OTHER POSSIBLE MODIFICATIONS TO OR EXTENSIONS OF CQR

One particularly intriguing modification would be to integrate other approaches into CQR. For example, we are now combining CQR with a group autoethnography approach (Råbu et al., 2019). Thus, rather than researchers conducting interviews with carefully selected participants, research team members write their own narratives, which are then analyzed by all the team members using standard CQR analyses (domains and core ideas within cases, categories and subcategories across cases). Such reflectivity on the part of team members allows for an in-depth exploration of complex topics (e.g., authenticity, effects of personal psychotherapy, boredom) across time.

Another combination approach would be, in conjunction with conducting CQR on interviews with therapists or clients or CQR-C, to conduct conversation analyses on text from therapy interviews (see Potter & Hepburn, in press). Furthermore, although we have not done so and thus have no first-hand recommendations, other researchers have successfully used CQR with data from focus groups (e.g., Hendrickson et al., 2002).

CONCLUSIONS

In this chapter, we described three ways (CQR-M, CQR-C, and QMA) in which CQR can be modified to fit the needs of the particular investigation. In addition, we noted that similar to Elliott and Timulak's (2021) generic model of qualitative research, CQR is flexible and can be modified in a number of ways.

9

CONCLUSIONS

In this final chapter, we first provide a summary of consensual qualitative research (CQR), along with its benefits and advantages, as well as its weaknesses and limitations. We then describe how CQR meets the standards recently put forth for conducting and reporting qualitative research. Finally, we draw conclusions about the method and present implications for its further development.

SUMMARY OF THE METHOD

CQR is a robust qualitative method that continues to gain popularity (Chui et al., 2012). In this method, the data analysis process is inductive, with findings emerging from the data themselves. The use of open-ended questions facilitates participants thinking deeply about the phenomenon under investigation, thereby eliciting rich data that consist of words rather than numbers. Contextual factors that may influence the data are taken into account, rather than being considered "noise" in the data. Instead of examining large numbers of cases superficially, CQR sample sizes are fairly small

https://doi.org/10.1037/0000215-009
Essentials of Consensual Qualitative Research, by C. E. Hill and S. Knox

(typically 13–15), enabling researchers to explore in depth the complexity of phenomena. The consensual element of CQR is central because it fosters multiple perspectives in reaching the best understanding of the data and also uses outside auditors to assess the accuracy and completeness of the primary team's analysis. During data analysis, researchers routinely return to the raw data themselves to ensure that they are accurately capturing participants' experiences.

In initiating a CQR project, researchers first choose a topic and review its literature. After selecting the research team, they develop and pilot the interview protocol, select and recruit from the target population, and conduct and transcribe the interviews. During data analysis, the researchers first develop domains from the transcribed data and then assign data to domains. They next create core ideas that capture the data in each domain for each case and then send this consensus version (i.e., the domains and core ideas for each case) to auditors for review. In the cross-analysis stage, the researchers identify themes (in categories and subcategories) that capture the findings across cases within domains and again send the emerging themes and categories (and the data—core ideas—that support them) to the auditors for review. Once the cross-analysis is finished, researchers look for patterns across domains, think about what the results mean, and prepare the manuscript for publication.

Benefits and Advantages of the Method

With CQR, researchers can examine phenomena deeply, hearing the voices and perspectives of those who have experienced the phenomenon of interest. As such, and via its use of open-ended questions, CQR facilitates the discovery of unexpected findings, rather than restraining or anticipating participants' potential responses (as would occur with participants completing standardized measures). CQR also enables researchers to build a short-term relationship (i.e., research alliance) with participants, which ideally enables the participants to feel safe disclosing what may well be difficult or uncomfortable experiences. Data collection in CQR is rigorous, with the use of a semi-structured protocol ensuring the collection of consistent domains of data from all participants, while also allowing researchers to explore more deeply other relevant areas that emerge from individual participants. Similarly, the data analysis process requires researchers to carefully examine both the trees (domains, core ideas) and the forest (cross-analysis) as the primary team and auditors reach consensus on the best understanding and interpretation of the data. The multiple perspectives inherent in CQR not only enhance the rigor of the method but also appeal to researchers' sense of collaboration and collegiality as they engage in the research process.

Limitations and Weaknesses of the Method

As is true of all methods, CQR is not without limitations or weaknesses. Though researchers seek to be aware of the biases or expectations they bring to a study, they may be more or less successful in doing so. As we demonstrated in one study (Ladany et al., 2012), two teams all trained in the same way arrived at somewhat different interpretations of the data, so clearly, biases and expectations do influence the research process. We argue, however, that our very humanness is what allows for the richness of results to emerge, in that we use ourselves and our perceptions to understand our participants more deeply, always checking to determine whether we have justification for our understanding according to the raw data. In addition, when we send them a draft of the manuscript, we ask participants to provide feedback regarding the degree to which we have accurately captured their experiences. Furthermore, it is important to acknowledge that in CQR, we are not seeking one single, objective, universally applicable "truth." Instead, for most of the phenomena in which we are interested, there are multiple truths depending on one's perspective. Thus, we seek to understand more deeply participants' experiences and perceptions, recognizing that we, as researchers, also influence the research process and results.

Another limitation relates to the recommendation to interview only people who are knowledgeable, able to articulate their experiences, and willing to be interviewed. People who have been traumatized, stigmatized, and are unable or unwilling to talk about such experiences are thus excluded from potential CQR studies because they cannot provide the kind of verbal data needed for CQR analyses. Such limitations may also restrict researchers from going into communities where there is minimal trust of outside personnel seeking to examine their experiences.

Although it is not specifically a limitation of the method, we also note that sometimes researchers do not develop incisive and probing interview protocols, fail to carefully select and recruit participants, and do not plumb the depths of participants' experiences in the interview, all of which lead to "thin" and superficial data. Research teams using CQR occasionally do not function harmoniously, which may both elicit discomfort and negatively affect data analysis. Finally, implementing the first two steps of the data analysis (i.e., domains, core ideas) can become tedious, which may then decrease researchers' investment in the project.

COMPARING CQR WITH OTHER METHODS

For quantitative researchers wanting to dip their toes into qualitative research, CQR can be attractive because of its clearly articulated procedures, as well as its emphasis on rigor, staying close to the raw data, describing rather than interpreting, and using multiple perspectives and auditors. In contrast, for some qualitative researchers, CQR may feel overly restrictive and rule-bound because it encourages researchers to stick closely to the raw data and not overly interpret or necessarily build theory.

Perhaps not surprisingly, because we started as quantitative researchers and still do both quantitative and qualitative research, we value rigor and replicability. We place ourselves right between the qualitative and quantitative empirical traditions, taking the best of both and integrating them so that we have a flexible way of representing complex phenomena.

METHODOLOGICAL INTEGRITY OF CQR

In their task force, Levitt et al. (2018) provided detailed standards for conducting and reporting qualitative research. These standards were adopted by the American Psychological Association (APA; 2018) and thus serve as criteria by which we can evaluate CQR. We assert that CQR, when faithfully and rigorously conducted and reported, meets these standards. In this section, we briefly justify our rationale for making this claim (see also Williams & Hill, 2012).

CQR clearly meets the standard of having as a foundation one or more undergirding research questions (e.g., How do clients experience therapist self-disclosure? What do therapists do when clients give them a gift?). CQR researchers also ground their research questions in the extant literature and provide a rationale for the importance of answering the questions. In addition, authors justify why CQR is an appropriate method for answering these questions (e.g., the method's generation of rich data from responses to open-ended questions asked of those who have experienced the phenomenon under investigation).

We also assert that CQR meets the standards related to participants, in that CQR authors describe participants' demographic information (e.g., age, gender, race, ethnicity, socioeconomic status) and other information relevant to the study (e.g., therapy or supervision experience) so that readers have a sense of who the participants are. Authors also delineate criteria for selecting participants (e.g., adults who have had at least 10 sessions of therapy, during which at least one therapist self-disclosure occurred) and recruiting the sample (e.g., contacted training directors of APA-accredited university counseling center internship sites). Given the influence of the interviewers and research team on the data, researchers also provide demographic information about the research team, along with other information relevant to the study (e.g., experience with the phenomena under investigation, biases and expectations related to the topic, experience using CQR). Furthermore, CQR authors detail the means of data collection (e.g., interviews, written responses to questions), the development of the data-gathering protocol (e.g., interview questions), and the rendering of the data into an analyzable format (e.g., transcribed from recorded interviews).

Similarly, researchers using CQR take care in describing the data analysis process, as suggested in the Standards, given that readers must understand how the data were examined to assess the trustworthiness of the findings. Authors describe the three stages of data analysis (i.e., domains, core ideas, cross-analysis), especially noting any variations in the method and the rationale for these variations. The team process and dynamics are also described, as well as the degree of agreement and disagreement among the team members as they engaged in data analysis and how any substantial disagreements were addressed.

When reporting and discussing the findings, researchers using CQR show how their results arose from the data themselves, as recommended in the Standards. For instance, they provide illustrative core ideas and/or evocative quotes from the interviews to demonstrate the basis for each finding. They also present findings in a logical and coherent manner that allows them to tell the most complete and compelling story about the data. In discussing their results, authors state the most central findings of the study, connecting them to the extant literature and addressing how the findings add to this literature base. Finally, they duly acknowledge the limitations inherent in their study and address implications for practice, training, and research.

Thus, we assert that if researchers follow the guidance provided in this and other texts about CQR (Hill, 2012; Hill et al., 1997, 2005), they can feel confident that their studies have met the Standards. We cannot, of course, guarantee that such adherence makes the data publishable because that potential outcome depends on the quality of the research questions, the study's findings, the quality of the manuscript, and the judgment of the reviewers of whatever journal to which the study is submitted.

IMPLICATIONS FOR THE FUTURE DEVELOPMENT OF CQR

All methods evolve as investigators develop better ways of conducting research. Indeed, we have changed CQR as we have gained experience with it since our first study (Rhodes et al., 1994). Hence, we fully expect that future researchers will identify additional ways of modifying CQR. We suggest the need to think carefully about how to select and recruit samples, how to train interviewers, how to complete the domains and core ideas in innovative ways so that researchers stay involved and immersed in the data, how to develop categories in the cross-analysis most effectively, how to look for patterns across domains, how to triangulate findings with results from other studies and methods, and how to effectively tell the story about the findings in the Discussion. We look forward to seeing how the method continues to evolve.

Appendix

EXEMPLAR STUDIES

Brown, C., Pikler, V. I., Lavish, L. A., Keune, K. M., & Hutto, C. J. (2018). Surviving childhood leukemia: Career, family, and future expectations. *Qualitative Health Research, 18*(1), 19–30. https://doi.org/10.1177/1049732307309221

Coren, S., & Farber, B. A. (2019). A qualitative investigation of the nature of "informal supervision" among therapists in training. *Psychotherapy Research, 29*(5), 679–690. https://doi.org/10.1080/10503307.2017.1408974

Hill, C. E., Kellems, I. S., Kolchakian, M. R., Wonnell, T. L., Davis, T. L., & Nakayama, E. Y. (2003). The therapist experience of being the target of hostile versus suspected-unasserted client anger: Factors associated with resolution. *Psychotherapy Research, 13*(4), 475–491. https://doi.org/10.1093/ptr/kpg040

Inman, A. G., Yeh, C. J., Madan-Bahel, A., & Nath, S. (2007). Bereavement and coping of South Asian families post 9/11. *Multicultural Counseling and Development, 35*(2), 101–115. https://doi.org/10.1002/j.2161-1912.2007.tb00053.x

Knox, S., DuBois, R., Smith, J., Hess, S. A., & Hill, C. E. (2009). Clients' experiences giving gifts to therapists. *Psychotherapy: Theory, Research, Practice, Training, 46*(3), 350–361. https://doi.org/10.1037/a0017001

Knox, S., Hill, C. E., Goldberg, J., & Woodhouse, S. (1999). Clients' internal representations of their therapists. *Journal of Counseling Psychology, 46*(2), 244–256. https://doi.org/10.1037/0022-0167.46.2.244

Knox, S., Hill, C. E., Knowlton, G., Chui, T., Pruitt, N., & Tate, K. (2017). Crying in psychotherapy: The perspective of therapists and clients. *Psychotherapy, 54*(3), 292–306. https://doi.org/10.1037/pst0000123

Ladany, N., O'Brien, K., Hill, C. E., Melinkoff, D., Knox, S., & Peterson, D. (1997). Sexual attraction toward clients, use of supervision, and prior training: A qualitative study of psychotherapy predoctoral interns. *Journal of Counseling Psychology, 44*(4), 413–424. https://doi.org/10.1037/0022-0167.44.4.413

Schlosser, L. Z., Knox, S., Moskovitz, A. R., & Hill, C. E. (2003). A qualitative examination of graduate advising relationships: The advisee perspective. *Journal of Counseling Psychology, 50*(2), 178–188. https://doi.org/10.1037/0022-0167.50.2.178

Vivino, B., Thompson, B., Hill, C. E., & Ladany, N. (2009). Compassion in psychotherapy: The perspective of psychotherapists nominated as compassionate. *Psychotherapy Research*, *19*(2), 157–171. https://doi.org/10.1080/10503300802430681

Williams, E. N., Soeprapto, E., Like, K., Touradji, P., Hess, S., & Hill, C. E. (1998). Perceptions of serendipity: Career paths of prominent women in counseling psychology. *Journal of Counseling Psychology*, *45*(4), 379–389. https://doi.org/10.1037/0022-0167.45.4.379

References

Adler, P. A., & Adler, P. (2002). The reluctant respondent. In J. F. Gubrium & J. A. Holstein (Eds.), *Handbook of interview research: Context and method* (pp. 515–535). Sage.

American Psychological Association. (2018). *Journal article reporting standards (JARS)*. https://apastyle.apa.org/jars/

American Psychological Association. (2020). *Publication manual of the American Psychological Association* (7th ed.). https://doi.org/10.1037/0000165-000

Berkeljon, A., & Baldwin, S. A. (2009). An introduction to meta-analysis for psychotherapy outcome research. *Psychotherapy Research, 19*(4–5), 511–518. https://doi.org/10.1080/10503300802621172

Berman, M., Hill, C. E., Liu, J., Jackson, J., Sim, W., & Spangler, P. (2012). Corrective relational events in the treatment of three cases of anorexia nervosa. In L. G. Castonguay & C. E. Hill (Eds.), *Transformation in psychotherapy: Corrective experiences across cognitive behavioral, humanistic, and psychodynamic approaches* (pp. 215–244). American Psychological Association. https://doi.org/10.1037/13747-012

Bikos, L. H., Manning, S. B., & Frieders, Z. J. (2019). Ready or not here I come: A qualitative investigation of students' readiness perceptions for study abroad/away. *International Perspectives in Psychology: Research, Practice, Consultation, 8*(2), 78–91. https://doi.org/10.1037/ipp0000105

Brown, C., Pikler, V. I., Lavish, L. A., Keune, K. M., & Hutto, C. J. (2008). Surviving childhood leukemia: Career, family, and future expectations. *Qualitative Health Research, 18*(1), 19–30. https://doi.org/10.1177/1049732307309221

Burkard, A. W., Knox, S., & Hill, C. E. (2012). Ethical considerations in consensual qualitative research. In C. E. Hill (Ed.), *Consensual qualitative research: A practical resource for investigating social science phenomena* (pp. 201–212). American Psychological Association.

Carr, E. C. J., & Worth, A. (2001). The use of the telephone interview for research. *Nursing Times Research, 6*(1), 511–524. https://doi.org/10.1177/136140960100600107

Chui, H. T., Jackson, J. L., Liu, J., & Hill, C. E. (2012). Annotated bibliography of studies using consensual qualitative research. In C. E. Hill (Ed.), *Consensual qualitative research: A practical resource for investigating social science phenomena* (pp. 213–266). American Psychological Association.

Cooper, H. (2016). *Ethical choices in research: Managing data, writing reports, and publishing results in the social sciences.* American Psychological Association. https://doi.org/10.1037/14859-000

Denzin, N. K. (1978). *The research act: A theoretical introduction to sociological methods.* McGraw-Hill.

Elliott, R. (1984). A discovery-oriented approach to significant events in psychotherapy: Interpersonal process recall and comprehensive process analysis. In L. Rice & L. Greenberg (Eds.), *Patterns of change* (pp. 249–296). Guilford Press.

Elliott, R. (1989). Comprehensive process analysis: Understanding the change process in significant therapy events. In M. J. Packer & R. B. Addison (Eds.), *Entering the circle: Hermaneutic investigation in psychology* (pp. 165–184). State University of New York Press.

Elliott, R., & Timulak, L. (2021). *Essentials of descriptive-interpretive qualitative research: A generic approach.* American Psychological Association.

Fischer, C. T. (2009). Bracketing in qualitative research: Conceptual and practical matters. *Psychotherapy Research, 19*(4–5), 583–590. https://doi.org/10.1080/10503300902798375

Gali Cinamon, R., & Hason, I. (2009). Facing the future: Barriers and resources in work and family plans of at-risk Israeli youth. *Youth & Society, 40*(4), 502–525. https://doi.org/10.1177/0044118X08328008

Gelso, C. J., Hill, C. E., Mohr, J. J., Rochlen, A. B., & Zack, J. (1999). Describing the face of transference: Psychodynamic therapists' recollections about transference in cases of successful long-term therapy. *Journal of Counseling Psychology, 46*(2), 257–267. https://doi.org/10.1037/0022-0167.46.2.257

Giorgi, A. (1985). Sketch of a psychological phenomenological method. In A. Giorgi (Ed.), *Phenomenology and psychological research* (pp. 8–22). Duquesne University Press.

Glaser, B. G. (1978). *Theoretical sensitivity.* Sociology Press.

Hayes, J. A., McCracken, J. E., McClanahan, M. K., Hill, C. E., Harp, J. S., & Carozzoni, P. (1998). Therapist perspectives on countertransference: Qualitative data in search of a theory. *Journal of Counseling Psychology, 45*(4), 468–482. https://doi.org/10.1037/0022-0167.45.4.468

Hendrickson, S. M., McCarthy Veach, P., & LeRoy, B. S. (2002). A qualitative investigation of student and supervisor perceptions of live supervision in genetic counseling. *Journal of Genetic Counseling, 11*(1), 25–49. https://doi.org/10.1023/A:1013868431533

Hill, C. E. (1990). Exploratory in-session process research in individual psychotherapy: A review. *Journal of Consulting and Clinical Psychology, 58*(3), 288–294. https://doi.org/10.1037/0022-006X.58.3.288

Hill, C. E. (2012). *Consensual qualitative research: A practical resource for investigating social science phenomena.* American Psychological Association.

Hill, C. E. (2020). *Helping skills: Facilitating exploration, insight and action* (5th ed.). American Psychological Association. https://doi.org/10.1037/0000147-000

Hill, C. E., Gelso, C. J., Chui, H., Spangler, P. T., Hummel, A., Huang, T., Jackson, J., Jones, R. A., Palma, B., Bhatia, A., Gupta, S., Ain, S. C., Klingaman, B., Lim, R. H., Liu, J., Hui, K., Jezzi, M. M., & Miles, J. R. (2014). To be or not to be immediate with clients: The use and perceived effects of immediacy in psychodynamic/interpersonal psychotherapy. *Psychotherapy Research, 24*(3), 299–315. https://doi.org/10.1080/10503307.2013.812262

Hill, C. E., Kellems, I. S., Kolchakian, M. R., Wonnell, T. L., Davis, T. L., & Nakayama, E. Y. (2003). The therapist experience of being the target of hostile versus suspected-unasserted client anger: Factors associated with resolution. *Psychotherapy Research, 13*(4), 475–491. https://doi.org/10.1093/ptr/kpg040

Hill, C. E., Kivlighan, D. M. III, Rousmaniere, T., Kivlighan, D. M., Jr., Gerstenblith, J. A., & Hillman, J. W. (2019). Deliberate practice for the skill of immediacy: A multiple case study of doctoral student therapists and clients. *Psychotherapy.* Advance online publication. https://doi.org/10.1037/pst0000247

Hill, C. E., Kline, K., Bauman, V., Brent, T., Breslin, C., Calderon, M., Campos, C., Goncalves, S., Goss, D., Hamovitz, T., Kuo, P., Robinson, N., & Knox, S. (2015). What's it all about? A qualitative study of meaning in life for counseling psychology doctoral students. *Counselling Psychology Quarterly, 28*(1), 1–26. https://doi.org/10.1080/09515070.2014.965660

Hill, C. E., Kline, K. V., O'Connor, S., Morales, K., Li, X., Kivlighan, D. M., Jr., & Hillman, J. (2019). Silence is golden: A mixed methods investigation of silence in one case of psychodynamic psychotherapy. *Psychotherapy, 56*(4), 577–587. https://doi.org/10.1037/pst0000196

Hill, C. E., Knox, S., & Hess, S. (2012). Qualitative meta-analysis. In C. E. Hill (Ed.), *Consensual qualitative research: A practical resource for investigating social science phenomena* (pp. 159–172). American Psychological Association.

Hill, C. E., Knox, S., & Pinto-Coelho, K. G. (2018). Therapist self-disclosure and immediacy: A qualitative meta-analysis. *Psychotherapy, 55*(4), 445–460. https://doi.org/10.1037/pst0000182

Hill, C. E., Knox, S., Thompson, B. J., Williams, E. N., Hess, S. A., & Ladany, N. (2005). Consensual qualitative research: An update. *Journal of Counseling Psychology, 52*(2), 196–205. https://doi.org/10.1037/0022-0167.52.2.196

Hill, C. E., Lu, Y., Gerstenblith, J. A., Kline, K. V., Wang, R. J., & Zhu, X. (2020). Facilitating client collaboration and insight through interpretations and probes for insight in psychodynamic psychotherapy: A case study of one client with three successive therapists. *Psychotherapy, 57*(2), 263–272. https://doi.org/10.1037/pst0000242

Hill, C. E., Nutt-Williams, E., Heaton, K. J., Thompson, B. J., & Rhodes, R. H. (1996). Therapist retrospective recall of impasses in long-term psychotherapy: A qualitative analysis. *Journal of Counseling Psychology, 43*(2), 207–217. https://doi.org/10.1037/0022-0167.43.2.207

Hill, C. E., Sim, W., Spangler, P., Stahl, J., Sullivan, C., & Teyber, E. (2008). Therapist immediacy in brief psychotherapy: Case study II. *Psychotherapy, 45*(3), 298–315. https://doi.org/10.1037/a0013306

Hill, C. E., Thompson, B. J., & Williams, E. N. (1997). A guide to conducting consensual qualitative research. *The Counseling Psychologist, 25*(4), 517–572. https://doi.org/10.1177/0011000097254001

Hiller, H. H., & DiLuzio, L. (2004). The participant and the research interview: Analysing a neglected dimension in research. *Canadian Review of Sociology and Anthropology, 41*(1), 1–26. https://doi.org/10.1111/j.1755-618X.2004.tb02167.x

Inman, A. G., Howard, E. E., & Hill, C. E. (2012). Considerations related to culture in consensual qualitative research. In C. E. Hill (Ed.), *Consensual qualitative research: A practical resource for investigating social science phenomena* (pp. 187–200). American Psychological Association.

Jackson, J. L., Chui, H. T., & Hill, C. E. (2012). The modification of consensual qualitative research for case study research: An introduction to CQR-C. In C. E. Hill (Ed.), *Consensual qualitative research: A practical resource for investigating social science phenomena* (pp. 285–303). American Psychological Association.

Janis, I. L. (1972). *Victims of groupthink*. Houghton Mifflin.

Kasper, L. B., Hill, C. E., & Kivlighan, D. M., Jr. (2008). Therapist immediacy in brief psychotherapy: Case study I. *Psychotherapy: Theory, Research, Practice, Training, 45*(3), 281–297. https://doi.org/10.1037/a0013305

Knox, S., Adrians, N., Everson, E., Hess, S., Hill, C. E., & Crook-Lyon, R. (2011). Clients' perspectives on therapy termination. *Psychotherapy Research, 21*(2), 154–167. https://doi.org/10.1080/10503307.2010.534509

Knox, S., & Burkard, A. W. (2009). Qualitative research interviews. *Psychotherapy Research, 10*(4–5), 566–575. https://doi.org/10.1080/10503300802702105

Knox, S., Burkard, A. W., Janacek, J., Pruitt, N. T., Fuller, S. L., & Hill, C. E. (2011). Positive and problematic dissertation experiences: The faculty perspective. *Counselling Psychology Quarterly, 24*(1), 55–69. https://doi.org/10.1080/09515070.2011.559796

Knox, S., DuBois, R., Smith, J., Hess, S. A., & Hill, C. E. (2009). Clients' experiences giving gifts to therapists. *Psychotherapy, 46*(3), 350–361. https://doi.org/10.1037/a0017001

Knox, S., Edwards, L. M., Hess, S. A., & Hill, C. E. (2011). Supervisor self-disclosure: Supervisees' experiences and perspectives. *Psychotherapy, 48*(4), 336–341. https://doi.org/10.1037/a0022067

Knox, S., Hess, S., Williams, E. N., & Hill, C. E. (2003). Here's a little something for you: How therapists respond to client gifts. *Journal of Counseling Psychology, 50*(2), 199–210. https://doi.org/10.1037/0022-0167.50.2.199

Kvale, S. (1996). *InterViews: An introduction to qualitative research interviewing.* Sage.

Ladany, N., O'Brien, K. M., Hill, C. E., Melincoff, D. S., Knox, S., & Peterson, D. A. (1997). Sexual attraction toward clients, use of supervision, and prior training: A qualitative study of psychotherapy predoctoral interns. *Journal of Counseling Psychology, 44*(4), 413–424. https://doi.org/10.1037/0022-0167.44.4.413

Ladany, N., Thompson, B. J., & Hill, C. E. (2012). Cross-analysis. In C. E. Hill (Ed.), *Consensual qualitative research: A practical resource for investigating social science phenomena* (pp. 117–134). American Psychological Association.

Levitt, H. M., Bamberg, M., Creswell, J. W., Frost, D. M., Josselson, R., & Suárez-Orozco, C. (2018). Journal article reporting standards for qualitative primary, qualitative meta-analytic, and mixed methods research in psychology: The APA Publications and Communications Board task force report. *American Psychologist, 73*(1), 26–46. https://doi.org/10.1037/amp0000151

Mahrer, A. R. (1988). Discovery-oriented psychotherapy research: Rationale, aims, and methods. *American Psychologist, 43*(9), 694–702. https://doi.org/10.1037/0003-066X.43.9.694

Marcus, A. C., & Crane, L. A. (1986). Telephone surveys in public health research. *Medical Care, 24*(2), 97–112. https://doi.org/10.1097/00005650-198602000-00002

McCauley, C. (1989). The nature of social influence in groupthink: Compliance and internalization. *Journal of Personality and Social Psychology, 57*(2), 250–260. https://doi.org/10.1037/0022-3514.57.2.250

McLeod, J. (2011). *Qualitative research in counselling and psychotherapy.* Sage.

Morrow, S. L. (2005). Quality and trustworthiness in qualitative research in counseling psychology. *Journal of Counseling Psychology, 52*(2), 250–260. https://doi.org/10.1037/0022-0167.52.2.250

Musselwhite, K., Cuff, L., McGregor, L., & King, K. M. (2007). The telephone interview is an effective method of data collection in clinical nursing research: A discussion paper. *International Journal of Nursing Studies, 44*(6), 1064–1070. https://doi.org/10.1016/j.ijnurstu.2006.05.014

Paterson, B. L., Thorne, S. E., Canam, C., & Jillings, C. (2001). *Meta-study of qualitative health research: A practical guide to meta-analysis and meta-synthesis.* Sage. https://doi.org/10.4135/9781412985017

Ponterotto, J. G. (2005). Qualitative research in counseling psychology: A primer on research paradigms and philosophy of science. *Journal of Counseling Psychology, 52*(2), 126–136. https://doi.org/10.1037/0022-0167.52.2.126

Potter, J., & Hepburn, A. (in press). *Conversation analysis.* American Psychological Association.

Råbu, M., McLeod, J., Haavind, H., Bernhardt, I. S., Nissen-Lie, H., & Moltu, C. (2019). How psychotherapists make use of their experiences from being a client: Lessons from a collective autoethnography. *Counselling Psychology Quarterly*. Advance online publication. https://doi.org/10.1080/09515070. 2019.1671319

Rennie, D. (1996). Commentary on "Clients' perceptions of treatment for depression: I and II." *Psychotherapy Research*, *6*(4), 262–268. https://doi.org/ 10.1080/10503309612331331788

Rhodes, R., Hill, C. E., Thompson, B. J., & Elliott, R. (1994). Client retrospective recall of resolved and unresolved misunderstanding events. *Journal of Counseling Psychology*, *41*(4), 473–483. https://doi.org/10.1037/ 0022-0167.41.4.473

Sánchez, F. J., Greenberg, S. T., Liu, W. M., & Vilain, E. (2009). Reported effects of masculine ideals on gay men. *Psychology of Men & Masculinity*, *10*(1), 73–87. https://doi.org/10.1037/a0013513

Schaefer, B. M., Friedlander, M. L., Blustein, D. L., & Maruna, S. (2004). The work lives of child molesters: A phenomenological perspective. *Journal of Counseling Psychology*, *51*(2), 226–239. https://doi.org/10.1037/0022-0167.51.2.226

Schielke, H. J., Fishman, J. L., Osatuke, K., & Stiles, W. B. (2009). Creative consensus on interpretations of qualitative data: The Ward method. *Psychotherapy Research*, *19*(4–5), 558–565. https://doi.org/10.1080/10503300802621180

Schlosser, L. Z., Dewey, J. H., & Hill, C. E. (2012). Auditing. In C. E. Hill (Ed.), *Consensual qualitative research: A practical resource for investigating social science phenomena* (pp. 135–144). American Psychological Association.

Schlosser, L. Z., Knox, S., Moskovitz, A. R., & Hill, C. E. (2003). A qualitative examination of graduate advising relationships: The advisee perspective. *Journal of Counseling Psychology*, *50*(2), 178–188. https://doi.org/10.1037/ 0022-0167.50.2.178

Shank, G. D. (2002). *Qualitative research*. Merrill, Prentice Hall.

Shuy, R. W. (2003). In-person versus telephone interviewing. In J. A. Holstein & J. F. Gubrium (Eds.), *Inside interviewing: New lenses, new concerns* (pp. 175–193). Sage.

Smith, J., & Nizza, I. (in press). *Interpretative phenomenological analyses*. American Psychological Association.

Spangler, P. T., Hill, C. E., Dunn, M. G., Hummel, A. M., Walden, T. T., Liu, J., Jackson, J. L., Ganginis Del Pino, H. V., & Salahuddin, N. M. (2014). Training undergraduate students to use immediacy. *The Counseling Psychologist*, *42*(6), 729–757. https://doi.org/10.1177/0011000014542835

Spangler, P. T., Liu, J., & Hill, C. E. (2012). CQR for simple qualitative data: An introduction to CQR-M. In C. E. Hill (Ed.), *Consensual qualitative research: A practical resource for investigating social science phenomena* (pp. 269–284). American Psychological Association.

Strauss, A., & Corbin, J. (1990). *Basics of qualitative research: Grounded theory procedures and techniques*. Sage.

Sturges, J. E., & Hanrahan, K. J. (2004). Comparing telephone and face-to-face qualitative interviewing: A research note. *Qualitative Research, 4*(1), 107–118. https://doi.org/10.1177/1468794104041110

Thomas, S. P., & Pollio, H. R. (2002). *Listening to patients: A phenomenological approach to nursing research and practice*. Springer.

Timulak, L. (2009). Meta-analysis of qualitative studies: A tool for reviewing qualitative research findings in psychotherapy. *Psychotherapy Research, 19*(4–5), 591–600. https://doi.org/10.1080/10503300802477989

Tuason, M. T. G., Taylor, A. R., Rollings, L., Harris, T., & Martin, C. (2007). On both sides of the hyphen: Exploring the Filipino-American identity. *Journal of Counseling Psychology, 54*(4), 362–372. https://doi.org/10.1037/0022-0167.54.4.362

Vivino, B. L., Thompson, B. J., Hill, C. E., & Ladany, N. (2009). Compassion in psychotherapy: The perspective of therapists nominated as compassionate. *Psychotherapy Research, 19*(2), 157–171. https://doi.org/10.1080/10503300802430681

West, M. A. (2004). *Effective teamwork: Practical lessons from organizational research* (2nd ed.). Blackwell.

Williams, E. N., & Hill, C. E. (2012). Establishing trustworthiness in consensual qualitative research studies. In C. E. Hill (Ed.), *Consensual qualitative research: A practical resource for investigating social science phenomena* (pp. 175–186). American Psychological Association.

Williams, E. N., Soeprapto, E., Like, K., Touradji, P., Hess, S., & Hill, C. E. (1998). Perceptions of serendipity: Career paths of prominent academic women in counseling psychology. *Journal of Counseling Psychology, 45*(4), 379–389. https://doi.org/10.1037/0022-0167.45.4.379

Index

About the Authors

Clara E. Hill, PhD, earned her doctorate at Southern Illinois University in 1974. She started her career in 1974 as an assistant professor in the Department of Psychology, University of Maryland, College Park, and is currently there as a professor.

She is currently the president-elect of the Society for the Advancement of Psychotherapy, and has been the president of the Society for Psychotherapy Research, the editor of the *Journal of Counseling Psychology*, and the editor of *Psychotherapy Research*.

Dr. Hill was awarded the Leona Tyler Award for Lifetime Achievement in Counseling Psychology from Division 17 (Society of Counseling Psychology) and the Distinguished Psychologist Award from Division 29 (Society for the Advancement of Psychotherapy) of the American Psychological Association, the Distinguished Research Career Award from the Society for Psychotherapy Research, and the Outstanding Lifetime Achievement Award from the Section on Counseling and Psychotherapy Process and Outcome Research of the Society for Counseling Psychology. Her major research interests are helping skills, psychotherapy process and outcome, training therapists, dream work, and qualitative research.

She has published more than 250 journal articles, 80 chapters in books, and 17 books (including *Therapist Techniques and Client Outcomes: Eight Cases of Brief Psychotherapy*; *Helping Skills: Facilitating Exploration, Insight, and Action*; and *Dream Work in Therapy: Facilitating Exploration, Insight, and Action*).

Sarah Knox, PhD, joined the faculty of Marquette University in 1999 and is a professor in the Department of Counselor Education and Counseling Psychology in the College of Education. She earned her doctorate at the University of Maryland and completed her predoctoral internship at The Ohio State University.

Dr. Knox's research has been published in a number of journals, including *The Counseling Psychologist, Counselling Psychology Quarterly, Journal of Counseling Psychology, Psychotherapy, Psychotherapy Research*, and *Training and Education in Professional Psychology*. Her publications focus on the psychotherapy process and relationship, supervision and training, and qualitative research. She has presented her research both nationally and internationally and has provided workshops on consensual qualitative research at both U.S. and international venues.

She currently serves as coeditor-in-chief of *Counselling Psychology Quarterly* and is also on the publication board of Division 29 (Society for the Advancement of Psychotherapy) of the American Psychological Association. Dr. Knox is a fellow of Division 17 (Society of Counseling Psychology) and Division 29 (Society for the Advancement of Psychotherapy) of the American Psychological Association.